D1521785

NOTE
GROUPING

NOTE GROUPING

A Method for Achieving Expression and Style in Musical Performance

by

James Morgan Thurmond

Professor Emeritus of Music Education
Lebanon Valley College

With a Foreword by
Weston H. Noble, Luther College

 JMT PUBLICATIONS
P.O. BOX 603/CAMP HILL, PENNSYLVANIA 17011

Second Printing, July 1983
Third Printing, November 1985
Fourth Printing, September 1987
Fifth Printing, January 1989
Copyright © 1982 by James Morgan Thurmond

Library of Congress Catalog Card Number: 81-90711

ISBN 0-942782-00-3

Printed by Jednota Press, Rosedale Avenue & Jednota Lane
Middletown, Pennsylvania 17057

TO THE MEMORY OF

ANTON HORNER

(1877-1971)

Gentleman, Horn Player, Teacher
Par Excellence

"We all know what *down and up* means,
but let's play as if there was only *up, up, up!*"
—*James Levine*
(Televised rehearsal of *La Traviata* on PBS.)

CONTENTS

The musical examples have been drawn by the author.

FOREWORD

Many of us in the field of music education can remember with unusual clarity certain learning experiences that have affected our teaching on an almost daily basis. They are not many in number, but the impact has been unusually profound.

Such was my summer with Robert Shaw and Julius Herford at San Diego State University in the summer of 1955. Among other musical concepts, I was exposed to a certain approach to phrasing which was to revolutionize my teaching of this most fundamental ingredient of musical performance. It was loosely termed "Baroque phrasing" or "crossbar phrasing." For six weeks I assimilated this new concept, realizing more and more it would be a part of every rehearsal I was to conduct the rest of my life.

For several years, I shared this different approach to phrasing in many clinics and workshops throughout the United States. It was always enthusiastically received. In May of 1961, I was adjudicating at the Buccaneer Festival, Corpus Christi, Texas, where one of my colleagues was Mr. James Kerr, band director at Wichita State University. He asked if I were aware of a Master's Thesis at the Catholic University in Washington, D. C. by James Thurmond entitled: *Note Grouping: A Means for Expression in Musical Execution.* I was not.

Upon returning home I sent for a copy of this dissertation. Upon its receipt I was thrilled. Here in print was exactly

11

the concept I had been exposed to by Robert Shaw and Julius Herford! In the almost twenty years that have followed, I have recommended to hundreds of directors all over the country that they purchase this special thesis! As a result it has been the most requested work in music at the Catholic University. If it has touched these hundreds of people in the magnitude I have experienced, it has had a profound influence upon music education everywhere!

To write the foreword of this book is a rare honor for me. The contents are so basic to every music teacher. May you be as rewarded as I have been every day since the summer of 1955!

—Weston H. Noble
Director of Music Activities
Luther College

PREFACE

In writing this book I have fulfilled a long-felt desire to put on paper my ideas concerning the emotional and expressive qualities of music, and how I believe they may be attained in musical performance. While the basic theories outlined in this work are not new to many, I believe the manner of their presentation will be, and that the chapters on *note grouping,* together with the instructions for the use of this concept, comprise a novel, practical, and heretofore unexplored approach to solving a most difficult problem—that of teaching students to play and sing with musicianship and expression.

All of the principles set forth herein have been tried and evaluated during many years of teaching, and have been found effective in developing style and aesthetic awareness. I am sure that any musician or music lover who carefully studies the contents of this volume will gain a new insight into the possibilities of determining exactly what makes the performance of one artist moving and forceful, and that of another, apathetic and mechanical. He will better understand why he is emotionally thrilled when he hears the warm, noble playing of an Isaac Stern or a Vladimir Horowitz, but is only mentally intrigued when he listens to a flawless, but cold technician.

I desire here to acknowledge my everlasting indebtedness to the late Mary Curtis Bok Zimbalist for the privilege of studying at the Curtis Institute of Music, where I first learned the elements of note grouping from the eminent musician and then principal oboist of the Philadelphia Orchestra, the legendary Marcel Tabuteau. My heartfelt gratitude is also extended to my teacher, the great Anton Horner, solo horn of the same orchestra for almost forty years and to whom this book is dedicated, for his unselfish, patient, and thorough instruction, especially in musicianship. From these famous men and others, including William Kincaid, principal flute, and Louis Bailly, violist extraordinary, I gained the critical outlook and knowledge of musical interpretation that has made the writing of this book possible. As a horn player, it was my good fortune while a student at Curtis to play under these artists in woodwind quintet and in many other chamber music ensembles, and to them, too, I have a debt I can never repay!

I wish also to thank the many persons who have encouraged me over the years to write this book. Among these are the late Dr. John Paul and Professor Conrad Bernier of the Catholic University of America, who made many valuable suggestions and read the manuscript of my Masters Dissertation from which much of the material herein is drawn. Finally I express my appreciation to my colleagues at Lebanon Valley College, Professor Frank E. Stachow, for his encouragement and support in finishing this project, and Professor George G. Struble, master teacher of the English language, for his many ideas and for checking the grammar.

This volume contains the accumulated experience and study of more than half a century of professional playing and teaching. I trust it will prove to be useful.

                                                            —*J. M. T.*

Camp Hill, Pennsylvania
July, 1981

NOTE
GROUPING

1
INTRODUCTION

Although many volumes can be found on the history, theory and appreciation of music, relatively few authors have attempted to set down in black and white any detailed rules or instructions for its *execution* or *performance*. The reasons for this anomaly are difficult to find. From earliest times great performers of music have been looked upon as geniuses by both musicians and non-musicians alike, and their ability to stir audiences with their playing or singing has too often been attributed to their musical gift or talent, rather than to their mastery of the principles or techniques of artistic performance. The true secrets of expressive playing[1] have been jealously guarded by the artists themselves and seldom passed on except to their most talented pupils—and then in most cases for a fee. Fear of competition has no doubt made many reluctant to part with their knowledge, while others, knowing that they have to teach for a living, have considered these secrets their stock-in-trade. All too

1. The words "playing" and "instrument," as used herein are of course synonymous with "singing" and "voice." All musical performance must necessarily be artistic and expressive to be worthy of being called art, and be governed by the same concepts and principles.

17

often musical artists who have great natural endowment are neither good teachers nor writers; consequently there has been very little written on the subject of artistic execution.

It is encouraging to note, nevertheless, that in recent years, principally in France and Switzerland, advances have been made in research into the methods and procedures of *teaching* expressive playing. This has resulted from the desire to help the many students who are technically proficient on their instruments but who lack the qualities of warmth and life in their playing so necessary to succeed as concert artists.

For years it was thought that this part of music could not be taught; that after a person had achieved technical mastery, he had to "find himself" *musically*. Mathis Lussy writes in the preface of his book *Musical Expression:* ". . . expression—the essence of music—seems to remain the property of a few gifted spirits, and brilliant execution is still far oftener met with than expressive playing."[2] Lussy's book is one of the pioneer works written to prove that expressive playing *can* be taught, and it is in pursuance of this same objective that this study has been made.

The Problem

The problem, of course, is to find, analyze and present a practical approach to the performance of music that will enable the executant to exhibit more expression, style and artistry in his playing or singing. After much study of the extant literature regarding interpretation, expression and musicianship, it has been found that there is an important relation between the way the *arsis* (or upbeat) is played, and the *movement* imagery present in the mind when one is listening to music. This imagery of movement, as will be seen later, actually does affect the kinesthetic nerve system and can cause the foot to tap, or incite in one the desire to dance. How many times have we heard someone say, "What a *moving* performance!", or, "I was so *moved* by his playing!"? The Reverend William J. Finn, director of the Paulist Choristers,

2. Mathis Lussy, *Musical Expression* (London: Novello and Co., 1931), p. iv.

was cognizant of this relationship when he wrote: "The mystery of music is in the upbeat."[3]

The approach recommended in this book therefore stems from the analysis and use of the *arsis-thesis* concept in musical execution as a means of achieving a high degree of movement, expression and style. In presenting this concept it is necessary to (1) trace briefly the evolution of rhythm and the metric foot, and how the importance of the thesis (or downbeat) developed; (2) show that arsis and motion are synonymous and that the quality of motion is the satisfying element in music; (3) present a system of grouping notes in an arsis-thesis succession (called NOTE GROUPING), which if used properly will increase the movement imagery engendered by music in the minds of both the performer and the listener; (4) set forth various applications of this system in pedagogy, performance, and conducting; (5) analyze, according to the theories presented herein, several performances of great artists taken from recordings; and (6) recommend a list of other recordings for further study and listening.

Importance

Is not one of the most important purposes of music or any other art to give *enjoyment?* It has been the experience of most of us, after having attended a concert, to hear members of the audience describe the artist's playing as "mechanical," "lifeless," "boring," "devoid of feeling," or some similar expression. Technique in itself is not enough to convey a message; there must be something more—movement, warmth, expression, aestheticism. In view of the paucity of literature on the subject of interpretation—especially *melodic* interpretation—it is believed that the following pages may be helpful to the student in achieving these qualities.

Elsewhere Father Finn has stated: "When and in what degree to accent? The instinctive reactions of men to poetic motion in its diverse forms require study by musicians who

3. William J. Finn, *The Conductor Raises His Baton* (New York: Harper and Brothers, 1944), p. ii.

would successfully answer this question."[4] Poetic motion in music—"the poetry of sound"[5]—is the important objective of the performer. He must learn what it is, how to recognize it, and how to attain it.

Related Works

As mentioned previously, the number of extant writings on expression in musical execution are few, and for the most part are confined to theoretical analyses rather than to the giving of practical instructions, or the outlining of effective procedures for achieving this quality of style in the playing of students. There are many so-called "methods," both instrumental and vocal, which give directions to guide the teacher in instructing pupils; however these rarely go into detail concerning expression or artistry in playing, and are usually devoted only to helping the student acquire technical and rhythmic mastery.

Perhaps the most complete analysis that has yet been made of the fundamentals of musical expression is set forth in the book quoted above of Mathis Lussy, *Musical Expression.*[6] In this work he divides the accents in music into three categories: metrical, rhythmical and expressive. After treating each type at length, Lussy states that the expressive accent is the most important, and supersedes the other two.[7] This book is a thorough study of the musical interpretations used by a number of great artists that Lussy heard during a period of many years, and should be read by every musician and music lover.

In *L'Anacrouse dans la Musique Moderne,*[8] Lussy discusses in detail every type of anacrusis found in music and stresses the importance of the upbeat in interpretation. To the author's knowledge there has been no English translation

4. *Ibid.,* p. 47.
5. Leopold Stokowski, *Music for All of Us* (New York: Simon and Schuster, 1943), p. 20.
6. Lussy, *op. cit.*
7. *Ibid.,* p. 125.
8. Mathis Lussy, *L'Anacrouse dans la Musique Moderne* (Paris: Librairie Fischbacher, 1903).

of this most important work, so unfortunately it is not easily available in the United States. For excellent material on the influence words have on music and expression, the little book by Émile Stiévenard, *Essai sur la Prosodie Musicale*[9] is recommended. Although it places particular emphasis on vocal music, instrumentalists will derive much knowledge from its study.

Probably the most scholarly work in this field by an American is *The Principles of Expression in Pianoforte Playing*[10] by Adolph F. Christiani, in which every phase of expression in piano playing is discussed. Many of Christiani's ideas are valuable only to pianists however, since they apply only to pianistic effects and problems. *Musical Interpretation*[11] by Tobias Matthay, the famous English pianist and pedagogue, mentions the mistakes he believed were made by famous composers—Chopin and Schumann in particular—in locating barlines when writing their music. Undoubtedly this will evoke some argument among those who believe that the great composers could make no mistakes; nevertheless it is excellent food for thought. The position of the barline is all-important in determining the expressiveness of the music.

There are many excellent dictionaries and histories of music in which material can be found relating to the development of the arsis and thesis. The standard work, of course is the monumental *Dictionary of Music and Musicians*[12] by George Grove, which is particularly valuable for a treatise on Greek rhythm; while in Emmanuel's *Histoire de la Langue Musicale*,[13] the evolution of the barline is outlined quite extensively, and many interesting facts are revealed concerning

9. Émile Stiévenard, *Essai sur la Prosodie Musicale* (Paris: Ménestrel-Heugel, 1924).

10. Adolph F. Christiani, *The Principles of Expression in Pianoforte Playing* (New York: Harper and Brothers, 1885).

11. Tobias Matthay, *Musical Interpretation* (London: Joseph Williams, 1914).

12. George Grove, *Dictionary of Music and Musicians,* ed. H. C. Colles, 4th Edition (Edinburgh: R. and R. Clark, 1940).

13. Maurice Emmanuel, *Histoire de la Langue Musicale* (Paris: Librairie Renouard, 1911).

the evolution of rhythm and meter. Dom Joseph Gajard's *The Rhythm of Plainsong*[14] is a most enlightening discussion of the rhythm of Gregorian Chant and places particular stress on the importance of the arsis and its rôle in musical interpretation.

There are several other significant volumes in which comment is made on the subject of phrasing and expression which for the most part have been included in the source material for the following chapters.

The Following Chapters

In order to approach the problem of achieving expressiveness in musical execution through the use of *note grouping* (grouping notes in *arsis-thesis* units) with an understanding of the historical background of this concept, the second chapter is devoted to a brief résumé of the *development of rhythm* as it applies to this method of performance. Since our modern conception of arsis-thesis is based on the position of the barline, some space is given to a discussion of the origin of this very important element of notation and how it affects the performance of music.

The third chapter investigates the affinity between *motion* and the expressive quality of music, and endeavors to show the principles of achieving the maximum amount of motion in the music played.

The fourth gives practical analyses of the concept of note grouping; while the fifth sets forth instructions for its use in pedagogy, plus a few of its many applications in composition, performance, and conducting.

The sixth chapter exhibits a number of passages taken from recordings of famous artists (those widely known as great interpreters of music) analyzed according to the note-grouping method presented in chapter four. These examples show that consciously or not, great musicians *do* group notes in a similar manner when playing, to achieve warmth, expression, and melodic motion.

14. Dom Joseph Gajard, *The Rhythm of Plainsong,* trans. Dom Aldhelm Dean (New York: J. Fischer and Bro., 1945).

The last chapter summarizes the conclusions reached after many years of teaching and studying this approach to musicality.

Appendix A is a list of recommended recordings that will be helpful in studying the note-grouping idea; in *Appendix B* will be found a *Glossary of Terms* defined as they are used in this book. For those who might enjoy reading the original French of many of the quotes, they are given in *Appendix C;* while *Appendix D* is an index of the musical examples used.

2 RHYTHMIC BACKGROUNDS

In order to understand the basic rhythmic concepts underlying the study of musical expression, it is necessary to investigate three facets of the evolution of rhythm: (1) the development of *motives*[1] as germ elements of rhythm and melody; (2) the development of *arsis* and *thesis*, and their classification as upbeat and downbeat; and (3) the genesis of the *barline.*[2]

Motive and Accent

Rhythm has always been an important part of human existence. The rhythms of day and night, of the seasons, of the change from wet to dry, of the ebb and flow of tides, and of breathing and walking are only a few of the cyclic phenomena by which all of nature is affected. These natural periodic

1. It will be shown later that the treatment of motives is the basis for the theory of note grouping as outlined in this book.
2. The "hierarchy" of the barline, which has led to the erroneous conception that the first beat in the measure should always be accented, has been largely responsible for the development of the style of playing characterized as "lifeless" or "mechanical," since it emphasizes *rhythm* and *meter* instead of the one element in music that is most important: *melody.*

25

changes found expression among primitive peoples through rhythmic movements, usually accompanied by some recurrent noise, like hand-clapping or the striking of sticks.[3] Later bodily motions developed into rude dances which were associated with chants of war, love, death, and religion.[4]

One of the oldest forms of chant that is still sung today is that traditionally used in the Jewish synagogue. These chants are of great antiquity and are probably of oriental origin. They are comprised of many different motives in which the beginnings of rhythm as we know it are found. Each motive (short musical figure or group of notes) has a different function. There are, for example, beginning motives and concluding motives. Originally they were classified according to their tonal, dynamic and time values. "In the Bible chants [used in the synagogue] the predominance of the motive is the most outstanding characteristic."[5]

In order to preserve the intonations used in singing the chants, *ear marks,* as they were called, were noted by the ancient Jews to indicate the rise and fall of the pitch and the curves made by the voice in singing a motive. Together with the ear marks, *hand signs* (Greek: *khéironomia*) were developed which were used by the teacher or leader to signify the progression of the melody up or down.[6] (A cheironomic method is used today by the monks of Solesmes, a village near Le Mans, France, in the conducting of Gregorian Chant.)[7] Later, names were given each detail marked by the voice and hand, and gradually written marks—diagrams of the hand movements—were invented to indicate them. The signs of the three principle tonal motions (today called *accents!*) were almost the same in all countries. Those still in

3. Waldo Selden Pratt, *The History of Music* (New York: G. Schirmer, Inc., 1927), p. 26.
4. Donald N. Ferguson, *A History of Musical Thought* (New York: Appleton-Century-Crofts, Inc., 1948), p. 8.
5. A. Z. Idelsohn, *Jewish Music in Its Historical Development* (New York: Henry Holt and Co., 1929), pp. 38-39.
6. *Ibid.,* p. 67.
7. Gustave Reese, *Music in the Middle Ages* (New York: W. W. Norton and Co., 1940), pp. 8-9.

common use today come from the Greek: *"acutus, circumflex,* and *gravis.''*[8] These three accents were indispensible characteristics of the ancient Greek language, as well as of Sanskrit and Chinese. They helped to indicate high or rising, rising-falling, and low or falling pitch respectively.

Spoken Greek was more musical than our language, and rose or fell according to the accents. The rhythm of the language also differed from ours in that there was *no dynamic stress* given to certain syllables. Instead the syllables that contained long vowels were approximately twice as long *in duration* as those with short vowels. "Greek speech, and especially Greek verse, had thus an intrinsic pattern of time—the primary basis of musical rhythm."[9]

The musician of today is likely to want to give the acute accent what would be a downbeat in our rhythm; however the rhythm of Greek was simply a pattern of long and short syllables (the same as in the spoken language) and the occurrence of the speech accents had no significance as far as the rhythm was concerned. Often the acute accent falls on what to us would be an upbeat or the short note after a dot, sometimes considered secondary or unstressed in our music. In Greek, however, "this note could not be secondary and was always accented."[10]

Arsis and Thesis

The terms *arsis* and *thesis* originated in the Greek drama where the leader of the chorus marked time for the dance with one foot encased in a shoe to which was attached a kind of clapper. This beat was not supposed to be heard by the audience, "nor were the *theses*— the 'foot falls' or strong elements of the poetic and musical measure—given any dynamic stress."[11]

8. Idelsohn, *op. cit.,* p. 67.
9. Ferguson, *op. cit.,* p. 33.
10. Curt Sachs, *The Rise of Music in the Ancient World, East and West* (New York: W. W. Norton and Co., 1943), pp. 259-260.
11. Ferguson, *loc. cit.*

28 *Note Grouping*

Curt Sachs writes:

> The metric accents in both poetry and melody followed the so-called quantitative principle; they materialized as long syllables or notes among short ones, not as strong among light beats . . . The two beats of all these feet were called *arsis,* lifting and *thesis,* dropping of the time-regulating hand or foot; in our words, upbeat and downbeat.[12]

Again in Grove's *Dictionary* we find:

> The Greeks called the weak beat *arsis* and the strong *thesis.* This is clear from Baccheios' *Catechism* (Meibom, p. 24):
> Q. What shall we say arsis is?
> A. The time during which the foot is raised when we are going to take a step.
> Q. And what is thesis?
> A. The time when it is on the ground. We need not go into such detail as the moment between arsis and thesis, for by its brevity, it escapes both eye (in the dance) and ear (in song).[13]

From the foregoing, then, we know that originally what we would call the *dynamic* accent (the stressed syllable) did not necessarily coincide with the thesis as in our modern poetry and song. In fact, if the accent occurred too often with the strong syllable of the poetic foot, the verse was held to be faulty.[14] For instance, the short syllable of the *iambus* (ᵕ ‒ , ♩ ♩ , weak-strong) was usually placed on what we would call the strong beat of the rhythm, thus: | ♩ ♩ |; instead of ♩ | ♩ ;[15] as we would write it today.[16]

---

12. Sachs, *op. cit.,* p. 263.
13. Grove, *op. cit.,* III, pp. 446-447.
14. Ferguson, *op. cit.,* p. 33.
15. If written | ♩ ♩ | today it would be called *syncopation* because of the misplaced accent, and would not be considered a normal rhythm.
16. Ferguson, *op. cit.,* p. 75, n. 4.

This shows that in ancient Greece the importance of the short syllables of the verse (in music, the smaller note-values) was recognized. This fact is important to remember later in this book when the author's theory of *note grouping* is presented; for the basis of this theory is that the arsis or weak note (upbeat) of the motive or measure (in an iambic meter) is more expressive musically than the thesis (downbeat), and that by stressing the arsis ever so slightly, the performance of music can be made more satisfying and musical.

Thesis, to the Greeks, meant the accented *part of the foot,* rather than merely the accented *note,* so that if one applies what they said of the foot to the entire measure, the following is obtained:

EXAMPLE 1

Thus, every unit in the measure down to the smallest foot— group of two in the case of the trochee (strong-weak)—is *thesis-arsis* in construction. This system is in fact a practical way of showing "that the accent (thesis) controls every section, small or great, of the phrase."[17]

The Romans also seem to have given rhythm importance, for evidence exists showing the use of recurring stress at equal divisions of time similar to the rhythmic scheme used in Western music.[18] By the fourth century the influx of alien tongues had gradually changed the principle characteristics of the strong element of Latin and Greek speech from one of *length* to that of *accent,* and it was inevitable that whenever the *thesis of the poetic foot* coincided with the *speech accent*

17. Grove, *op. cit.*
18. Reese, *op. cit.,* p. 52.

a *dynamic* stress should occur.[19] This gradual change in the structure of the poetic foot slowly increased the accented rhythm in the music written to accompany it, resulting in a dynamic ictus or stress occurring on the thesis or strong element of the foot.

There was only the verse to indicate the musical rhythm before the twelfth century. Exact time was not desired in plain-chant, so it was in the hymns and sequences that the rhythms of verse gradually became the basis for the mensuration of music. The musicians of the period took the meter for their verses from the many varied ones that had been used by the Greeks, and of these the rhythmic meters that gradually came to be preferred were the following: *trochee* (– ⌣ = ♩ ♪) ; *iambus* (⌣ – = ♩ ♪) ; *spondee* (– – • ♩. ♩.) ; *dactyl* (– ⌣ ⌣ = ♩. ♩ ♩) ; *anapaest* (⌣ ⌣ – = ♩ ♩ ♩.); *molossus* (– – – = ♩. ♩. ♩.); and *tribrach* (⌣ ⌣ ⌣ = ♩ ♩ ♩).[20]

It is believed that these seven "rhythmic modes," as they are called, were used by the troubadours and trouvères in singing their melodies, and although this music is originally written in plain-chant notation, the fact that a great number of the pieces are dancing songs makes it fairly certain that they must have been performed "with definite beats definitely grouped."[21] Another fact giving credence to this theory is that compositions have been found not only in the old notation, but also, apparently due to their popularity, in later editions which show time values according to the rhythmic modes.[22] These modes, according to medieval authorities, were all in ternary rhythm (e.g., dactyl and anapest) as shown above, and it was not until later in the thirteenth and fourteenth centuries that binary rhythm or time evolved. One can easily see from the note-values diagrammed above

19. Ferguson, *op. cit.*, p. 37.
20. Ferguson, *op. cit.*, pp. 74-75.
21. Reese, *op. cit.*, p. 206.
22. *Ibid.*, p. 272.

how naturally the *upbeat* developed from the arsis (short note) and the *downbeat* from the thesis (long note).

The Barline

The stress which was given to the thesis occurred regularly in the rhythmic modes, and it naturally followed that the first differentiation in note-values came as a result of imitating this poetic rhythm on the musical staff. It was only a step further to consider each thesis a point of rest, and the regular occurrence of this stressed syllable as a rhythmic factor grouping the notes of the poetic foot together and dividing the composition into equal portions. These portions later developed into measures; each characterized by the occurrence at the beginning, of the thesis, and separated in order to more visibly show these portions by the *barline*.

Other influences which led to the development of the *barline* are interesting, especially the part played by the dance. During the dance revival of the latter part of the sixteenth century, the leaps and kicks of the dancers of the Middle Ages disappeared, and the fact that the feet were kept more closely to the ground tended to emphasize the rhythm. In the early seventeenth century the *carrure* (quadrature, or balancing of phrases in four or eight measures) appeared:

". . . in the seventeenth century the quadrature haughtily takes its place: its coarseness offers advantages. It indicates the steps with a useful clearness to the dancers. It adjusts itself to accommodate the initial beats—in each measure [of the music]—of which the dancer is fond."[23]

Slowly, the stress given to the first rhythmic beat, so necessary to the dancers, was instrumental in causing this beat to become the most important one in the measure, and must surely have influenced its being placed immediately after the barline.

Another influence was the need that arose for a means to make the reading of music easier. As long as all music was

23. Maurice Emmanuel, *Histoire de la Langue Musicale* (Paris: Librairie Renouard, 1911), pp. 433-434.

monodic (in a single-voice style, as in Gregorian Chant), or
note against note (as in *organum*), there was no real need for
a barline, since division of the phrase was made by the verse
accents; however when one part began to be more florid than
the rest, it was necessary to superimpose the parts in score
form in order to show how the voices were to combine.[24] This
practice naturally led to the use of the barline running the full
length of the score—from top to bottom.

In the seventeenth century the comprehension and the
tradition of the choral art began to become lost, principally
because of the difficulty of performing the compositions.
Counterpoint had become so elaborate that sometimes as
many as thirty or more parts were written. In the Renaissance
the barline did not exist; consequently there were no fixed
marks in the music to guide the director of the choir: "each
chorister had no other recourse for keeping his place than his
feeling."[25] The writing was so inexact that beating time for
the musicians was very difficult, and as a result the players or
singers of the seventeenth century, "when they tried to
rehearse the works of the sixteenth century, more through
reverence no doubt than by choice, soon found themselves
prevented from reading them."[26]

It is believed, therefore, that in addition to the development of the barline for rhythmic reasons, the measure also
appeared in notation because it was needed "in a certain era
to read the numerous parts which rose tier upon tier (gradually one over the other) in scores";[27] it being necessary to
have some means of enabling the reader to see the position of
the notes in relation to each other, and of aiding the conductor to beat the meter. Today, even though one cannot play
music without the barline, it should be realized that it is only
a means to help us to better execute the duration of the
notes.[28]

Before the advent of the barline (circa 1600 A.D.) the

24. Reese, *op. cit.,* p. 269.
25. Emmanuel, *op. cit.,* p. 434. (French: *touchement.*)
26. *Ibid.*
27. Stiévenard, *op. cit.,* p. 18.
28. *Ibid.,* p. 19.

divisions of a composition were indicated by the repose at the end of the phrase and parts of phrases. In this way no vertical line separated the melodic line; and one read, played, or sang the musical *idea* or *phrase,* and not the measure (as one observes many musicians doing today). The over-accentuation of the first beat in the measure (or thesis) in serious music, which is at the root of unexpressive playing, can be said, then, to have arisen primarily from a legitimate need for an excess of rhythmic stress in dance music (the same as in popular music today). It is obviously a serious mistake, however, to consider all music as if it were written for the dance, and transfer this stress to every downbeat or every thesis simply because it is first in the measure!

3 MOTION IN MUSIC

Movement and Rhythm

In ancient Greece, the arts were classified into two groups: (1) architecture, sculpture, and painting; and (2) music, poetry, and the dance. The Greeks thought that the "beautiful," the goal of all art, was achieved by the first group in a *state of repose;* that the different elements composing this group—juxtaposed in *space*—were perceived at one particular moment of their existence. In the second, however, the "beautiful" was realized in a *state of movement;* by a succession of its elements during *time.*[1] It is this quality of *movement,* or motion, presented during the succession of its elements, that is the basis of the enjoyment that we receive from listening to music.

James L. Mursell, who achieved eminence as a writer in the field of musical psychology, stated:

> We know that tonal-rhythmic patterns are very closely associated with the voluntary musculature, and very importantly influence its action. Again and again, in the

1. Dom André Mocquereau, *Le Nombre Musical Grégorien* (Rome, Tournai: Desclée & Cie., 1908), I, p. 26.

literature, the relationship between music and the sense of voluntary movement is emphasized. In a very elaborate study of musical enjoyment, Weld finds that whenever visual imagery is present during listening, it is always *movement* imagery.[2]

This movement imagery,[3] created in the mind by a succession of musical tones, gives rise to the sensation we know as *rhythm.* The following paragraph, written by one of the leading musicologists of this century, is significant:

> In psychology, musical *rhythm* depends upon the fact that tones presented in temporal sequence are perceived as having not only pitch, loudness, quality, and duration, but also *movement.* Movement is so exactly *progression from one note to another in a melody* that the term is a literal use of the word. And yet the objective stimulus which produces the sense of movement is a movement, not through space, but rather through *time.*[4]

Why can't the four *physical* properties of musical tone (pitch, loudness, quality, duration) alone create rhythm? Why is motion also necessary? Because "rhythm is in the intellect."[5]

An analysis of the above characteristics of tone shows why this is true. If a group of notes are played that are exactly equal in *intensity,* but different in duration, such as ♩ ♪♩ ♪♩ ♪, an impression of rhythm will occur due to the feeling of *movement* from the short note to the long note. Here the generating cause of rhythm cannot be intensity, for the degree of loudness is equal throughout; and since rhythm has been produced *without intensity*, this property of tone can be eliminated as a causative factor.

In like manner, a series of notes *alike in duration,* such as

2. James L. Mursell, *The Psychology of Music* (New York: W. W. Norton & Co., 1937), pp. 38-39.
3. It is movement imagery that causes one to beat his foot when a stirring march is heard!
4. Glen Haydon, *Introduction to Musicology* (New York: Prentice-Hall, Inc., 1941), pp. 85-86.
5. Gajard, *op. cit.,* pp. 18-19.

♩ ♩ ♩ ♩ ♩ ♩, will give an impression of rhythm if one or more of them are *intensified* (accented): ♩ ♩ ♩ ♩ ♩ ♩; due again to the *movement* from each non-accented note to the following accented note. Duration, therefore, must also be ruled out as a generator of rhythm.[6]

It is, of course, obvious that neither *pitch* nor *quality* (timbre) can be rhythmic since they both exist in a tone that has no movement whatsoever! In fact, rhythm is not composed of sound at all, since it can be perceived without the ear. Can one not watch a pendulum without hearing the tick of the clock, and still get an impression of rhythm? In this connection, it is known that the Greeks had to watch the bodily motions of the dancers in addition to hearing the music in order to feel rhythm; for to them, music and dance were synonymous.[7]

Sister Mary Goodchild, O.P., in her book on Gregorian Chant says:

> Saint Augustine called rhythm "the art of beautiful movement," and this art is strikingly illustrated in the chant, for while the rhythm is free from the restrictions of mathematical measurement, it is alive with beautifully ordered movement.[8]

Although the music of Gregorian Chant is basically different from that of our familiar rhythmic kind, and is not divided into actual measures, it is not felt to be arrythmic. We have become so used to hearing music accented in regularly recurring elements and in strictly measured time "that we have almost come to believe that the word 'rhythm' implies a succession of thumps. Properly however, it means *motion* . . . the effort to escape such mechanical regularity is one of the most striking features of contemporary music."[9]

6. Gajard, *Ibid.*
7. *Ibid.*
8. Mary Antoine Goodchild, *Gregorian Chant* (New York: Ginn and Co., 1944), p. 10.
9. Donald N. Ferguson, *A History of Musical Thought* (New York: Appleton-Century-Crofts, Inc., 1948), pp. 47-48.

It can properly be stated, then, that *rhythm* is synonymous with *movement*—"ordered movement."[10] In fact the word "rhythm" comes to us from the Greek: *rhythmos,* meaning "measured motion";[11] and Plato's definition was: "Rhythm is order in movement . . ."[12]

Motion and Expression

If rhythm is dependent upon motion, it follows that the more motion there is in music the more rhythm,[13] and consequently the more *expression;* since "expression" in music—the same as in any art—may be defined as a quality or impression of *movement,* warmth and life resulting from rhythmic change, like that which characterizes any living thing. Music that is mechanical, cold, lifeless; that leaves us *unmoved;* "has lost its spontaneity and human quality."[14] The principal difference between a thing alive and a dead or inanimate one is the ability to *move,* and it is precisely this same quality that distinguishes expressive playing from dull "execution." Just as a human being is characterized by the rhythm of *living*—by his heart-beat, breathing, and walking, by his eating, sleeping, and working—all different kinds of motion; so must music that is alive also have its rhythms:[15] the pulse of the meter, the ebb and flow of phrases, dynamic contrasts, the rise and fall of moving note groups.[16]

10. Gajard, *op. cit.,* p. 10.
11. *Webster's Collegiate Dictionary* 5th Edition (Springfield: G. and C. Merriam Co., 1946), p. 857.
12. Justine Ward, *Gregorian Chant* (Washington: Catholic Education Press, 1923), p. 10.
13. It must be emphasized that "rhythm," as used here, means the ebb and flow of the music itself, and not strong and weak beats, differentiation of note values, or meter.
14. Leopold Stokowski, *Music for All of Us* (New York: Simon and Schuster, 1943), p. 22-23.
15. See note 13.
16. In a larger sense, of course, the *arsis* may comprise the entire anacrusis of a "rhythm" or phrase "section," in other words, the entire *motion-creating,* "up-swing" part of the phrase (rise) as opposed to the "down-swing" or restful part (fall).

From this analysis it is apparent therefore, that if one endows his execution with the maximum amount of motion (i.e., achieves a strong perception of motion in the minds of his audience) he has at the same time performed with the greatest possible amount of *expression.*

The problem therefore that faces the serious student of music can be reduced to the following: What can be done to enable one to obtain more motion in musical performance, so that rhythm (not meter!), life and expression will become essential attributes of the interpreted music? Obviously, the answer to this question may be found first by analyzing the construction of music in order to *find the factors that create the perception of motion,* and second, by devising a formula or method that may be used when playing or singing that will *bring these factors into bolder relief.*

Importance of the Arsis

As mentioned before,[17] a perception of rhythm or motion[18] can be engendered in the mind of the listener by playing either alternating tones of different lengths or tones of unequal dynamic stress. In each case the motion-creating factor is the *progression* from short to long tones or from unaccented to accented ones or vice versa. When for a number of reasons[19] the barline gradually developed, it was placed before the long or accented notes (theses), making each *measure* "thetic" in a sense—that is, beginning with a thesis and ending in an arsis. As a result this development has led to the notion that the *first* note in the measure (or beat) should be considered the *most important* and should be given the most *accent;* the principal reason being that this note is *first!* The consequence of this prominence has been that the theses are overaccented in performance and the arses neglected.

This practice is opposed to the principles of poetry and

17. See pages 36-37.
18. It has been shown that in aesthetic feeling these two terms are synonymous
19. See page 31f.

rhythm handed down to us by the Greeks,[20] and limits the
progressive function of melody[21] (the most important and
necessary element of music)[22] as it is illustrated in the compositions of the masters. In melody, the arsis, or in a larger
sense, the anacrusis,[23] is the most important part of the
motive, *rythme,* phrase, or measure; for it is this portion that
"progresses" from one harmonic structure to another[24]
(passing notes), and usually contains the only notes that are
different from the harmony. Moreover, the metric pulse normally gives a certain amount of stress to the thesis, or initial
beat in the measure, and to increase this prominence by emphasizing it, *solely because it is first,* makes the musical result
stiff, mechanical, and over-accentuated. Also, the harmonic
pattern of the music usually falls on the thesis of each measure or beat, and any thetic accentuation of the melody tends
to blend it into the harmony so that its true melodic rôle in
the music is obscured, resulting in a loss of clarity and

20. See page 27f.
21. Percy Goetschius writes that "melody is a manifestation of
tone-relations in horizontal or *progressive* association, whereas
harmony associates tones vertically or simultaneously." (*Theory
and Practice of Tone Relations* [New York: G. Schirmer, Inc.,
1892], p. 14). (Italics by the author.)
22. Of the three basic elements of music—melody, rhythm and
harmony—the first, melody, is alone indispensable; and of the
three, is the most important. One may have music without harmony or rhythm, but not without melody. In interpretation (or
performance) therefore, melody must always be given the most attention. James L. Mursell states that "melody always may be, and
in its essence *always* is, entirely independent of harmony . . . harmony depends on melody, not melody on harmony . . ." (*The
Psychology of Music* [New York: W. W. Norton & Co., 1937], p.
389.).
23. Anacrusis (anglicized from the Greek: *anakrousis*) means
the first or "upswing" portion of a motive or phrase, beginning on
an arsis and ending on a thesis, and may contain one, two or more
notes. (See *Ex. 5,* page 43).
24. Except of course in the case of accented passing notes, syn-
copations, appogiaturas, etc., and even here the thesis (or harmonic structure) can be considered as merely being delayed; the
non-harmonic notes being arsic in nature.

musical expression (movement). This is due principally to the fact that when the theses are accented, the true melodic mission of the arses is restrained and they fade into the valleys between the thetic "thumps." Consequently their *progressive* function is not perceived by the listener.

Another factor besides the placement of the barline that has contributed to this "worship" of the downbeat is the method that has evolved of writing and printing the notes themselves in a *thesis-arsis pattern.*[25] This puts a thesis not only at the beginning of every *measure,* but at the beginning of every *beat,* signifying to the uninitiated that this thetic note is important, *only because it strikes the eye first!*

To overcome this visual stumbling block (i.e. the printing of notes in beats with their tails joined thus: ♩♫ ♫♫ ♫♫ ♩ ‖ , rather than printing them ideally: ♪♫♫♫♫♫ ♩ ‖!, as shown in *Ex. 2*),

EXAMPLE 2

Hugo Riemann, the great German musicologist, advocated the use of what he called "reading marks," which are small vertical marks (') placed in the music to separate the motives and phrases. In addition, he advocated "separation of tails or bars of notes when possible" (as shown immediately above).[26]

25. See *Ex. 1,* page 29.

26. Hugo Riemann and Carl Fuchs, *Practical Guide to the Art of Phrasing* (New York: G. Schirmer, 1890), p. 16.

To illustrate, the phrase:

EXAMPLE 3

would be written thus by Riemann:

EXAMPLE 4

It can be quickly seen however, that the use of this system would delay and confuse the immediate recognition of the meter, so necessary in sightreading, and make too difficult the combination of voices when writing a score. The procedure outlined by the author in the next chapter is more practical, and still closely parallels the ideas of Riemann.[27]

Grove's *Dictionary* discusses "upbeat and offbeat" as follows:

> The Greeks had a word 'anakrousis' which they used as we talk of "striking up" a piece of music. Of this the French made *anacrouse* while the Germans use *Auftakt* to express what we call "off-beat." The cry of nearly all animals, including man, proceeds from an unaccented note (generally low) to an accented one (high), and it is therefore in the nature of things that much music should begin on the offbeat anacrusis, a doctrine associated with the names of Westphal and Riemann.
>
> The offbeat in this sense is not necessarily limited to the last note of the bar[*sic*]. It would include, for instance, the three preliminary notes of the 'Marseillaise,' but eventual-

27. For purposes of comparison, this same phrase as *grouped* by the author according to the system presented in Chapter 4 would be: [music notation] . Obviously, this is a simpler solution of the same problem. (See Chapter 4.)

ly it includes all phrases that do not begin with the first of the bar.[28.]

For example:

EXAMPLE 5

The value of the anacrusis in interpretation is attested to by Lussy as follows:

> Anacruses play an extraordinary rôle in music: they are the soul of the sections [*rythmes,* or half-phrases] and, as a result, of *execution.* They have the faculty of producing the *pathetic accent,* that of modifying the *general movement* [of the music], the dynamism, that is to say the intensity, the *nuances* [shades of color] of a musical phrase, and of inspiring great deeds.[29]

Another famous French theoretical scholar, Auguste Gevaert, states:

> While modern theory recognizes only thetic measures, beginning with the downbeat and enclosed within two barlines, ancient writers also admitted *anacrusic* measures beginning with the upbeat. They even used to say that this last combination seemed to them the most regular; in fact, they always spoke of the arsis before the thesis, which, from a certain point of view, is very logical, every percussive beat being necessarily preceded by an upbeat.[30]

In the beginning, when first learning to read music, a child must first read each separate beat and the notes or rests that comprise that beat. Later he must be trained to read by measures, and to see *at a glance* all the beats in each measure;

28. Grove, *op. cit.,* V, p. 424.
29. Mathis Lussy, *L'Anacrouse dans la Musique Moderne, op. cit.,* p. 2.
30. Auguste Gevaert, *Histoire et Théorie de la Musique de L'Antiquité* (Gand: Annot-Broeckman, 1881), II, p. 22.

otherwise he will never become a good sightreader. All too often, however, students continue to read by measures far longer than they should and do not learn to read by motives and phrases, or in other words, read "over the barline." This practice of reading by measures results in wind players breathing at every barline, pianists practicing one measure at a time, and in the lack of ability to recognize the true motives, phrases and periods of the music, never realizing that, as J. Alfred Johnstone says in his book, *Touch, Phrasing and Interpretation:*

> . . . the most usual normal rhythm is the rhythm of the upbeat followed by the downbeat . . . is it any wonder that those who look from the note following a barline to the note ending a measure; from strong to weak; often miss all the delicate motival punctuation of their music, and jog along quite satisfied with the mechanical swing of metrical monotony. If, therefore, the interpretation of music is to be intelligent and interesting, the player must cease to regard the barlines as the dividing points of his music, and must instead turn his attention to its motives and phrases.[31]

In speaking, one uses words before phrases, and phrases before sentences. It is much the same in music: one thinks first of its motives, and then its sections, phrases and sentences. The movement from one note to another creates the motive; and "just as in walking one must first raise the foot before putting it down, so too the motive normally begins on an upbeat (upbeat: lifting, *arsis;* downbeat: lowering, *thesis*). Of course there are many motives which begin with the downbeat, but they are exceptions involving an artificial foreshortening of the normal upbeat motive . . ."[32] In other words, in most cases where motives or phrases seem to begin on a thesis or downbeat, there should be an *imaginary* arsis *understood* immediately before the initial note. In the examples, the imaginary arsis has been indicated by an **A** in parenthesis—(A).

31. J. Alfred Johnstone, *Touch, Phrasing and Interpretation* (London: William Reeves, 1909), p. 33.
32. Hugo Leichtentritt, *Musical Form* (Cambridge: Harvard University Press, 1951), p. 5.

Sometimes whole measures are really upbeats or anacruses. Take for instance the following theme from one of the *Songs Without Words, Op. 67, No. 6* by Mendelssohn:

Mendelssohn - *Song Without Words, Op. 67, No. 6*

EXAMPLE 6

At first glance one would think that this theme started on the downbeat; however since it doesn't, the first measure is more important *melodically* than the second, for the *first measure is arsic!*

Another writer observes that "the rhythms [sections of a phrase] beginning on the strong beat are relatively rare";[33] and Alec Robertson observes that the acknowledged master of all contrapuntalists, J. S. Bach, wrote motives and phrases that almost exclusively *begin on the arsis.* He writes "that the down-beat is not of its nature strong . . . this may be seen in the correct phrasing of the well-known *G Minor Organ Fugue* [of Bach] . . .

J. S. Bach - *Organ Fugue in G Minor*

etc.

EXAMPLE 7

"Even if the organ were capable of percussive accent its use would be unnecessary, as the accents in Bach's passage from movement to repose are beautifully marked merely by the melodic elevations [high to low], and it is the upbeat and not the downbeat that stands out."[34]

It must be understood that in addition to being a great composer, Bach was a master of the organ, and knew how to fuse the arts of composition and execution so that they complemented each other. He wrote his motives and phrases so

33. Louis Anciaux, *Le Rythme, Ses Lois et Leur Application* (Tamines [Belgique]: Duculot-Roulin, 1914), p. 37.
34. Alec Robertson, *The Interpretation of Plain Chant* (London: Oxford University Press, 1937), p. 19.

they would "sound"; and the fact that they do, is indisputable evidence of the correctness of his methods.

Walter Piston, eminent American composer, writes in his book on counterpoint:

> The sense of motion forward to the next downbeat, imparted by the anacrusis, seems to be continually present in melodies possessing unmistakable rhythmic vitality, such as those of J. S. Bach. It is as though each downbeat serves in turn as a springboard for the start of another anacrusis, ever renewing the life of the melody.[35]

A few examples will show that not only Bach but all the great masters instinctively felt the power of the anacrusis. In the *Sonata, Op. 13,* the *Pathétique,* Beethoven ties the first dotted sixteenth-note to the opening quarter in order to emphasize the expressive qualities of the anacrusis leading to the third beat. The opening note merely states the key and there would be no point in repeating it; however the first thirty-second, while it retains the same pitch, has something *melodically* important to say:

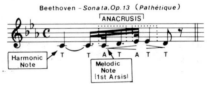

EXAMPLE 8

To cite another instance, the first theme of the *Andante* of the same composer's *Symphony No. 1* makes this one of the most expressive of slow movements for the reason that each motive is set into the three-eight time so as to give prominence to its most expressive portion—the anacrusis:

EXAMPLE 9

35. Walter Piston, *Counterpoint* (New York: W. W. Norton & Co., 1947), p. 34.

It is suggested that Beethoven might have slurred the last arsis in the measure to the thesis (4) (and in the following two measures), so that the increased stress (*tenuto*), properly given in interpreting the first of a group of slurred notes, would add to its arsic intensity. In a broader sense, the second eighth should be included in the anacrusis, but in this melody its anacrusic quality is minimal due to the third eighth being slurred, except of course at (1), (2) and (3). Notice that the final **C** is slurred to the preceding **B-flat**, bringing out the arsic quality of the third beat (the following **A**) by separating it from the note before it.

Many examples from the works of the masters of musical composition could be given as further proof of the fact that the anacrusis is the basic generator of motion in the motive[36] or phrase. The reader is referred especially to the symphonies of Johannes Brahms in which almost every motive and theme is built on the arsis-thesis concept. Three of these themes are particularly expressive due to their anacrusic construction, and it is fitting to close this chapter with their analysis.

In the *Andante* of the *Symphony No. 1 in C Minor,* the theme of the oboe is particularly moving in its emotional effect due to the three anacrusic eighths which are repeated in each motive, and then given greater definition and eloquence at the close by slurring them and transferring the following thesis to the strings. Note particularly how Brahms divides the stems at (1) to emphasize the importance of the anacrusis:

EXAMPLE 10

36. Is it not significant that the word *motive* is derived from the same stem as *motion*?

Then in the last movement of the same work, the heroic
theme for first violins in **C** major:

EXAMPLE 11

The nobility of this passage is due in no small degree to
the expressiveness of the anacruses preceding the first and
third measures. The anacruses preceding the second and
fourth measures have less emotional impact and have not
been marked. Throughout this symphony, as mentioned
before, almost all of the motives, sections and phrases succeed each other by beginning on the upbeat and ending on
the downbeat.

The last example to be quoted is from the *Symphony No.
3 in F Major*. It is the poignant violoncello (and horn) solo in
the third movement which is marked *Poco allegretto:*

EXAMPLE 12

In interpreting this theme at the opening of the movement, the conductor usually holds the opening anacrusis a bit
longer than written in order to emphasize its eloquent and
moving qualities. It is especially appealing at (1) and at (2),
and again at (3) and (4) due to the aesthetic sensitivity and
movement of the anacruses.

In the next chapter a *method* is presented that, if used
and taught properly, will insure that the anacruses receive the
importance that is necessary if they are to perform their appropriate function—that of endowing the melody with
movement, emotion and life!

4 NOTE GROUPING

Fundamental Theory

In order that the reader may understand more completely the reasoning that underlies the theory of *note grouping*, the first part of this chapter will be devoted to a summary of the fundamental concepts on which this method is based.

It was pointed out in Chapter 3 that the arsis or anacrusis, whichever it may be, is the motion-creating factor in the motive or phrase; and that the great composers must have felt this to be true, since the majority have written their music in a manner that highlights the importance of the anacrusis. Proper recognition of this importance by the artist will insure that in performance the composition will be phrased correctly and with ease; for if, with few exceptions, the *true* motives and phrases begin with anacruses, one has only to phrase from one anacrusis to the next thesis *before* the next "motive-beginning" anacrusis! *Phrasing,* or "punctuation" in music, in the opinion of the author, is almost synonymous with expression. Therefore if proper significance is given to the anacrusis, and the thetic portions of the measure are not stressed, phrasing will be more correct and consequently the expressiveness of the music will be enhanced.

The origin of phrasing is not known; however Frederick Dorian asserts that the art, as an applied discipline in the performance of music, is young. The following paragraphs from his book, *The History of Music in Performance* are interesting:

> D.C. Turk in his *Clavierschule* (1789), feels entitled to boast of priority in the employment of phrasing ... It is in a somewhat humorous manner that Turk introduces his analogy between tone and word language, with the following illustration:
>
>> 'He lost his life not, only his property.
>> He lost his life, not only his property!'
>
> Obviously the wrong punctuation changes the meaning of the sentence to the point of distortion. Turk justifiably concludes that the same danger of wrong punctuation exists in music.[1]

The problem of where to punctuate—where singers and wind players should breathe, where string instrumentalists should bow—is a neverending one. The enigma is the location and immediate recognition of the proper boundaries of the motives and phrases, and the consequential task of executing the music so that these phrases are properly defined, and are heard by the listener according to their relative importance in the passage as a whole. This is one of the most perplexing of the many hurdles that must be negotiated by the musical performer and one that the author believes is greatly clarified, if not solved, by the use of the note-grouping method.

In approaching the analysis of the problem of where to punctuate or phrase, it is important to remember that in music, as in literature, the perception of the art progresses from the motive (which is comparable to the syllable or word in prose) to the phrase; and then to the sentence, period, and finally to the work as a whole.

---

1. Frederick Dorian, *The History of Music in Performance* (New York: W. W. Norton and Co., 1942), pp. 160-161.

Vincent d'Indy vividly reminds us of this in the following words:

> In certain arts, *architecture, sculpture, painting,* the whole appears before the detail: the assimilation of the work progresses from the *general* to the *particular.* In the others, *literature, music,* the detail strikes one first and leads to the appreciation of the whole: the assimilation progresses from the *particular* to the *general.*[2]

To paraphrase the above: if one were observing the cathedral of Notre Dame in Paris, he would first see the structure as a whole and then proceed to examine the famous stained glass windows and other of its noble features in particular; however if one were listening to the *Symphony No. 5* of Beethoven, he would necessarily first hear the motive:

EXAMPLE 13

and only then would it be possible for him to progress to the next motive, the next phrase, period, theme, movement, and finally the complete work. It is therefore imperative in phrasing that attention be focused first on the *smallest items,* the figures or motives, and then on the larger ones.[3]

As discussed earlier, the motive in its smallest form may consist of only two notes, the first usually being the arsis and the second the thesis.[4] If these notes are examined more closely, it will be found (to repeat a previous statement) that each has a particular function to perform: the former to create action or movement, the latter to be the result of that action—a point of rest, or relaxation. What is the explanation of this phenomenon?

2. Vincent d'Indy, *Cours de Composition Musicale* (Paris: Durand et Cie., 1912), p. 17.

3. J. Alfred Johnstone, *op. cit.,* pp. 42-43.

4. Occasionally one finds motives that start on the thesis, especially in marches. This is no doubt due to the necessity for accentuation of the first beat of the measure to keep the feet of the marchers together.

   Mathis Lussy believes that the factor generating the feeling that the upbeat or arsis pulsation has a life-giving
characteristic, and the downbeat a quality of relief from tension, can be traced to the physiological mechanism of
breathing.[5] In breathing there are two movements—inspiration and expiration. Inspiration personifies action; expiration, repose. The former is symbolized by the upbeat and the
latter by the downbeat. A striking word picture of this most
plausible explanation is given by Lussy in another passage
from his treatise, *L'Anacrouse dans la Musique Moderne:*

> To take and to give, such is the physiological function
> of man. The first thing that a being does on coming into
> the world is to *inspire,* to take in air. The last thing that he
> does is to *expire,* to render the last sigh: this is the end,
> supreme repose.[6]

   Lussy also believes that respiration furnishes a key to the
origin of binary and ternary rhythms. When a person is
awake and in movement, the breathing is in *binary* rhythm:

EXAMPLE 14

And when he is *asleep* or at complete rest, the respiration is in
ternary rhythm—the exhalation being approximately twice
as long as the inhalation:

EXAMPLE 15

5. Lussy, *op. cit.,* p. 67.
6. *Ibid.*

One has only to observe an individual who is in deep slumber to appreciate the significance of this observation.

It is clear from the above that a complete respiration (inhalation-exhalation) provides a prototype of the musical motive—or note group, whether in duple or triple rhythm. In the following pages the author has *bracketed* all note groups according to the above principle: inhalation-exhalation or arsis-thesis ($\overline{\text{AT}}$).

Unfortunately the system of writing and printing music in use today provides no means for showing the true outlines of the motive or phrase. It is necessary of course due to the complexity of modern musical compositions, and the large number of staves in the scores, that the metric scheme be immediately apparent to the reader; consequently measures, notes, and groups of notes, from the smallest to the largest, are written and printed according to the *meter* and not the motive or phrase. For example, the following melody is shown in (a) as it is now written, and in (b) as it would be written (and played) if the boundaries of each of the *motives* were to be properly shown:

EXAMPLE 16

Seldom however, are motives recognized and played as shown in (b) above (except by accomplished musicians or those who are inherently musical), accounting to a large degree for the mechanical, lifeless execution so often heard by one who is aware of the musical style that *should* be used. *Note grouping* provides a short cut to the immediate recognition of the germ motives, and consequently the sections and phrases; for are they not merely combinations of the motives?

In the analysis of note grouping presented to the reader at this point, it seems logical to divide discussion into three phases. First, to examine the *patterns* (a term chosen by the author) of *THESIS-ARSIS* construction as they appear in *manuscript* or *printed* music; second, to present the writer's method of *note grouping,* or scheme of grouping notes according to their inherent motival character, which will reveal the *ARSIS-THESIS* construction; and third, to cite various examples exhibiting a few of the many applications of the note-grouping theory.

Thesis-arsis PATTERNS in printed music

In *Example 1,* Page 29, it was shown that each *unit* (i.e. note or beat) in a measure of simple, binary time, as *written* or *printed,* is composed of two parts; the first of which is a *thesis,* the second an *arsis* (together constituting a *trochee,* — ‿); the *metrical* length of each being *one-half* of the unit in question. For example, a whole-note, as printed, contains two half-notes, the first a thesis and the second an arsis; a quarter-note contains two eighth-notes, the first a thesis, the second an arsis. For the purpose of this analysis this arrangement will be called a thesis-arsis *PATTERN.* (Each pattern will be designated **P** in the examples.)

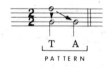

T   A
PATTERN

EXAMPLE 17

If the above principle is carried further, down to the smallest note-value, the following paradigm is obtained:

EXAMPLE 18

Looking more closely, it can be seen that the *faster* music is written, the *larger* the note-values that are used; and the *slower* the music the *smaller* the note-values. In an *adagio* passage one will usually find eighth, sixteenth, and thirty-second notes, while in *presto* the note-values will be mostly quarter, half and whole-notes.

In studying *Example 18,* be aware that each *pattern* is composed of *two smaller* patterns. This observation is important to remember later during the discussion of *note groups* (arsis-thesis in construction).

In *Example 19* a similar design can be observed in *simple ternary time* (as printed), except that the basic measure unit is divided into *three* parts (beats) instead of two, the first of which is a *thesis,* and the second and third *arses,* (constituting a dactyl, —⌣ ⌣). This unit will be called a *thesis-arsis-arsis PATTERN.* For instance, in a *printed* measure of three-four time, the *pattern* of the three quarter-notes in each measure would be as follows:

EXAMPLE 19

However, if each quarter in *Example 19* were *further* divided, the *pattern* of each division would henceforth be the same as for each unit in binary time: *Thesis-arsis:*[7]

EXAMPLE 20

In *slow compound* time, with either two, three, four or more beats to the measure, the *pattern* of the component *divisions* of each dotted note-value is, of course, the same as that of the principal *beats* in *simple ternary* time: *Thesis-arsis-arsis.*[8] For example, in six-eight time (six beats):

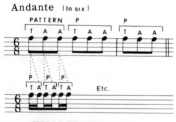

EXAMPLE 21

7. See *Example 18,* p. 55.
8. Further subdivision would be as in *Ex. 20*—binary.

In *fast compound* time, with two, three, four or more beats in each measure, the component *divisions* of each dotted-value (or beat) form the same pattern (as shown immediately above): *thesis-arsis-arsis* or *thesis-arsis* as the case may be:

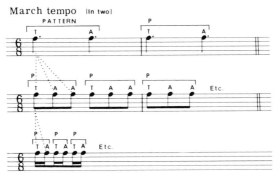

EXAMPLE 22

The patterns in nine-eight (**A**), and twelve-eight time (**B**), follow the same arrangement:

EXAMPLE 23

From the foregoing diagrams it can be seen that the *printed patterns* of the *NATURAL* divisions of all *plain* note-values are *thesis-arsis* and of all *dotted* note-values, *thesis-arsis-arsis*.

The patterns for duple and triple (binary and ternary) *ARTIFICIAL* divisions are the same as those for the normal divisions illustrated above; however in artificial divisions of *more than three parts,* each pattern is constituted as follows: First note—thesis; remaining notes—arses:[9]

EXAMPLE 24

In the *sextuplet,* the pattern would of course depend on the speed of the composition:

EXAMPLE 25

9. All notes in a printed *pattern* that occur after the thesis are arsic; that is, they compose the anacrusis of the next thetic note-value or unit. This anacrusis includes all the smaller values contained within the larger ones, as will be explained later.

A *double triplet* would also be patterned according to the tempo:

EXAMPLE 26

Arsis-Thesis NOTE GROUPS

Even Note-values[10]

NATURAL DIVISION

Binary Rhythm

The foregoing section (pages 54-60) showed how the *patterns* occur in written or printed music; however it has been explained previously that the *thesis-arsis* arrangement of the *pattern* is not the true succession of pulses, and that this arrangement is contrary to all aesthetic and natural laws, and the rules of melody; it being necessary (to again repeat!) only for convenience in reading the music so that the meter may be instantly clear, and in enabling one to write or read a score in which numerous staves are combined, one over the other.

Therefore if one is to execute music properly, with emotion and expression, he must *mentally suppress* the *thesis-arsis pattern,* while in the process of reading the music, and superimpose (again mentally!) an *arsis-thesis* GROUP, in

---

10. The terms *even* or *uneven* do not apply to *patterns* since they are all printed the same and are readily apparent to the eye. *Note groups* comprising *uneven* note-values are more obscure and are discussed later in detail. See p. 68.

order that the active or moving note (which must always be thought of as being *first* in the group) is *followed* by the passive or restful one—and *always in this succession!*

This is a most delicate procedure, and if done improperly may easily lead to playing that sounds quite ludicrous. The line that can be drawn between excellent playing and true artistry is very difficult to define. Each of us knows when we are stimulated by the expressive playing of a performer, but few of us can explain the *reasons* for this stimulation. In employing this concept, therefore, one should not think that it can be used without the musicianly good taste that goes hand in hand with excellent technical development, artistic temperament and scholarly analyzation of the music.

In using note grouping, one *does not accent* the groups; one does not *emphasize* the first note of a group; one conceives the music differently. Instead of thinking and SEEING *patterns,* the way notes are printed: THESIS ARSIS (⌐TA⌐); the performer thinks and SEES *note groups,* the way the notes speak *musically:* ARSIS-THESIS (⌐AT⌐)! As a result, expressiveness will appear—*even in spite of the performer!*

To be sure, if one does bring out the first note of a group (⌐AT⌐) slightly more than the rest, isn't that because of its natural importance as the premier note in the group? In fact, the only justification a musician can give for accentuation of the first note of each *pattern* is that it is first—in the beat or in the measure— and that he *sees* it first! After the first few years when the beginner has learned to read music (by recognizing beats), there no longer is any reason for accenting this first note.

If there is a desire to intensify a particular arsis or anacrusis for *musical* reasons to make the passage more expressive, is this not sensitive musicianship? It has been shown that the arsic quality is the only *expressive* quality in music (other than accentuation), so the thing to do is to "lean" on the arses ever so slightly. This does not mean mechanical, regular accentuation of the first note of *every group.*

Later in this book instructions for teaching note grouping will be given, and like all "methods" for teaching a new

system, these directions will recommend a slight emphasis of
the boundaries of the groups in order to overcome habits
that have been built up from years of playing the wrong way
(accenting the first note of printed patterns). However after a
student is familiar with the true outlines of the note groups
and the expressive qualities of the music, it is still up to him to
properly coordinate motives, phrases, sentences into a ra-
tional whole; playing or singing each according to its inherent importance in the musical passage. *There is no short
cut to artistry!* Note grouping can help—the same as technique, analysis, and temperament—however it is no
panacea; it must be used by an intelligent, sensitive performer capable of great imaginative powers. If this concept
only helps to prevent mechanical over-accentuation of the
theses, it shall have done its part!

At this point it is suggested to the reader that for the time
being he cease thinking about *patterns*. Although perception
of patterns at all times is necessary for sight reading since
they permit instant recognition of the meter and the all-
important beat; they are however, in essence, the antithesis
of expressive performance. The playing of note groups actually results in one playing "off the beat" or "between the
beats," since the true motive or note group consists of the
latter part of one beat plus the first part of the next. Even
though one has "graduated" from reading and thinking
metrical patterns, it is still of course necessary to be aware of
the beat at all times in order to participate in ensemble playing of any kind. The result is an inner consciousness at all
times of the beat and pulse of the meter, while at the same
time purposely playing note groups "between the beats" to
make the music "come alive" and express the emotion one is
trying to convey to the audience.

At first, to assist the uninitiated eye to single out the correct groupings of arses and theses, it has been found advantageous to place small brackets (⌐‾⌐) over each particular
group (the same as was done for each *pattern* in the foregoing section), always in the succession *arsis-thesis* (⌐AT⌐). This
group may be either a motive, or, in a group of only two
notes, sometimes only a sub-motive. For example, in the

melody shown in *Example 27,* brackets are placed over every motive (group) and sub-motive (figure).[11] It is apparent that every *two* of the smaller groups combine to form *one* of the next larger groups:

EXAMPLE 27

This phenomenon can readily be observed in its application to even note-values; but in its application to *uneven* ones, the grouping is somewhat more obscure. Further in this chapter note-values that are different in length will be fully explained.

If the procedure of grouping each arsis to its thesis (as

11. See *Ex. 16,* p. 53.

shown in *Ex. 27)* is extended throughout the series of note-values in binary meter, the following result will be obtained:[12]

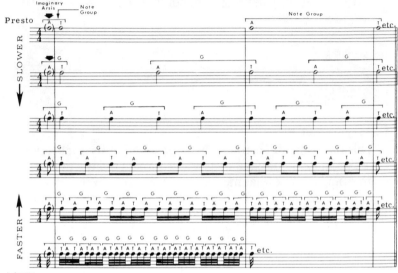

EXAMPLE 28

Again attention is called to the fact that in *slow* music more of the smaller note-values will be in evidence and in *fast* music the larger ones. By combining the smaller groups to form the next larger ones and then combining these to form the next larger, and so forth, the true outlines of the phrase, sentence and period are finally achieved. For instance, here is the first subject of the fourth movement of the *Concerto in B-Flat Major* for piano and orchestra by Johannes Brahms, grouped from the smallest group (sub-motive or figure) to

12. Compare with *Ex. 18,* p. 55.

the period, showing how the complete melody is built from many small units (groups):

EXAMPLE 29

It is only by mentally taking cognizance of the smallest groups that the whole period can be correctly expressed; just as in a sentence of prose each syllable of each word must be pronounced correctly, and the words punctuated properly, to form intelligible thought; for, as we have learned, music is a temporal art and must be perceived in time, motive by motive, until the entire composition is heard. It follows also that if the smallest groups are correctly recognized and played, the sections, phrases, and sentences will also become apparent and will fall into their proper places; each acquiring its proper degree of importance in the work as a whole.

When reading in note groups (always *arsis-thesis* in form), the perception of the arsis as the *first* note in the group automatically tends to increase its importance, and accords it its true value in the motive or phrase as the *action-creating* or *motion-creating* agent.[13] The thesis, appearing *second,* is unconsciously given less attention and its *melodic* importance decreases in accordance with its rôle as a note of repose or rest. In this way the lilt of the music is made more manifest, and the motion generated by the movement from arsis to thesis is continuous throughout the phrase, giving it life and meaning.

Example 28, page 64, showed how note-values in duple or quadruple *simple* time are grouped. Component eighth-

13. The same as the importance given to the *first* note of the *printed pattern* (simply because it is first) has given rise to mechanical interpretation of melody through over-accentuation of the thetic and metrical qualities of the music.

notes in duple **(a)** or quadruple **(b)** *compound* time, would be
grouped *arsis-arsis-thesis* ($\overline{AAT}$), as follows:

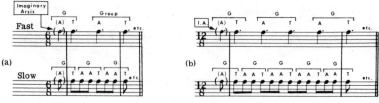

EXAMPLE 30

Ternary Rhythm
Notes in triple *simple* time **(a)**, and triple *compound* time
(b), would be grouped:

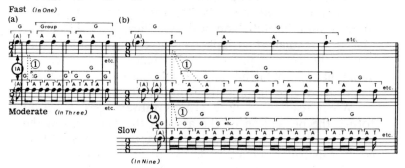

EXAMPLE 31

The reader will observe that in *ternary* time the smaller
note-groups may be *combined in threes* (*Ex. 31*, (1)), in
accordance with the larger basic note group (composed of
beats) in the measure (the same as smaller note groups in
binary time are *combined in twos* to make larger groups),
since this is the group that must logically evolve from the fu-
sion of the smaller groups if the *tempo should become faster.*
When melodies begin on the thesis, there is always an *imaginary* arsis understood. Many times the arsis is not apparent but actually occurs in another voice of the harmony. Imaginary arses will be shown in the examples **IA**, or will be *in-
closed in parentheses:* **(A)**.

When mentally grouping notes, as outlined above, the number (or value) of notes composing a group depends on the *speed* of the composition. If the tempo is *presto* the note groups will be composed of large note-values (which increases the number of smaller notes inherent in each group), and sometimes even whole measures are grouped (e.g., when the composition is in a fast tempo and conducted in one beat per measure).[14]

For instance in *L'Apprenti Sorcier* by Paul Dukas:

EXAMPLE 32

the measures are grouped in threes,[15] while in the first movement of Beethoven's *Fifth Symphony:*

EXAMPLE 33

the measures are grouped in fours. This grouping, of course, changes as the compositional structure (form) of the movement changes.

ARTIFICIAL DIVISION

All of the discussion so far regarding note grouping has been relative to *natural division* of note-values. *Artificial division* is governed by the same principles: all *arses* in each

14. See *Ex. 6*, p. 45.
15. See *Ex. 42*, p. 75.

note group (all notes in the beat or measure, *after the first*) are grouped with the following thesis:

EXAMPLE 34

Uneven Note-Values

Binary Rhythm

The foregoing presentation has been concerned mainly with the primary arsis-thesis groups (sub-motives or motives) in which all note-values are *equal*. However music is seldom restricted to this type of notation, for it is in variety that much of the charm of this art lies, so that for the greater part of music the interpreter is concerned with notes of *unequal* time value.

In grouping notes of different lengths it is necessary at first glance to mentally apply the note-grouping principles simultaneously to all the *component parts* (or units) of each note (whether these parts are visible or not) in the terms of both the *smallest* and the *largest* note-values exhibited in the particular passage. For example, the following rhythm should be thought of as containing *all* the small and large groups that are applicable:

EXAMPLE 35

In this way the exact importance of each note in the phrase becomes apparent immediately, again depending upon the speed of the music. The *slower* the piece the more the *next smaller* note-values must be visualized; the *faster,* the more one should be conscious of the *next larger* ones. To put it another way: if the player is thinking note groups in quarter-notes, (𝄴 ♩ ♩ ♩|♩) he should also simultaneously be thinking note groups in eighths (𝄴 ♫ ♫ ♫ ♫|♪) if they exist anywhere in the passage. If he is thinking in half-notes (¢ ♩ ♩|♩ ♩|♩), he should also think note groups in quarters (¢♩ ♩ ♩|♩) and perhaps also in eighths (¢ ♫♫ ♫♫ ♪), and so on.

The same procedure is applicable in the case of *tied* notes: all the component note groups (subdivisions) should be visualized mentally as one plays. For example in the following rhythm one should think of the first (thetic) eighth (1) as having its arsis (an eighth note) in the preceding quarter (4), and

the second (arsic) eighth (3) as grouped according to the
rhythmic diagram in eighths. The downbeat quarter (2)
should have an *imaginary* quarter-note arsis (shown in parentheses, **(A)**) felt as an upbeat or preparatory beat. The
rhythmic subdivision is shown immediately below the staff:

EXAMPLE 36

"The Happy Farmer" from *Album for the Young, Op.
68, No. 10,* of Schumann, is an excellent theme for analysis,
for the groupings are easily recognized. As shown in the
rhythm schematic below the music, the first eighth is
grouped with the imaginary first eighth of the following
dotted-quarter, while the second group is in the right hand
accompanying figure. Two of the smaller groups combined
make one of the larger groups. At first glance, the pianist will
play the groups as shown in the schematic at (2); however this
action is wrong because it retards the movement toward the
barline (as shown by arrows). When grouped as shown at (1),
the life of the melody *begins* with the dotted-quarter instead
of *ending* with it. The whole piece "progresses," and a scintillating "musical" effect occurs. Instead of dotted-quarters
being musically "dead," they are very much alive! If this
melody were played on a wind instrument, each dotted quarter would be slightly *intensified* toward the end of the note.
Scherchen, in his *Handbook of Conducting,* writes of a
"crescendo of intensity" as opposed to a *dynamic* crescendo. Perhaps this "crescendo of intensity" applies here.[16] This
is due to the *progressive* feeling of the underlying eighths in
the right hand. This manner of thinking will also insure the
sostenuto (sustaining) of long notes in melodies instead of

16. Herman Scherchen, *Handbook of Conducting* (London:
Oxford University Press, 1935), p. 80.

the *diminuendo* so often heard in the playing of wind and string instruments.

EXAMPLE 37

The first note of a group (arsis) always *progresses* to the second note (thesis). It is this *progression* that causes the sensation of movement. If the above passage had not been written so perfectly all the life and joyousness would be missing. It is the constant lift of the first note of each group that makes this little piece so captivating. How trite and lacking in spirit it would be if it were written contrary to the natural note groups:

EXAMPLE 38

Even though it were played perfectly (with note grouping!), it would present quite a different character. Compare this passage with the quotation of Turk on punctuation (page 50). How the position of the barline changes things!

Most of the time the short note-values composing the component groups within the long notes of a melody appear elsewhere in the music, as in this little piece (*Ex. 37*). The pianist must always be on the alert, for these smaller notes help to influence the character of the larger ones. Often the orchestral musician has difficulty properly playing a long, sustained melodic note. If he, too, will think of the smaller note groups *within* the long note (subdivide mentally), he will

parallel the musical activity elsewhere in the orchestra and
the long tone will assume the life, meaning and intensity it
should possess. Needless to say, he will breathe in the right
place!

    To illustrate further, observe the following passage for
clarinet and bassoon in the second movement of Brahms'
Symphony No. 3:

EXAMPLE 39

    If the clarinetist and bassoonist feel the three component
quarters as shown in the rhythm schematic, they will have no
trouble putting expression into the dotted-half, if only to
slightly intensify it. The first **A** is an arsis, so it should be
pressed a little, however the first quarter of the dotted-half is
the following thesis, so it should just be *lightly touched!* The
second quarter of the dotted-half is an arsis; consequently
the note intensifies almost imperceptibly before the following triplet. This also provides the necessary *sostenuto* of the
slow, sustained melodic note. The last two notes of the triplet
are grouped with the following quarter ($\overline{AAT}$); the first note
being the thesis of two previous *imaginary* arses understood
as part of an *imagined* triplet in the dot (third beat) of the
preceding dotted-half. The following **D** is also a thesis and is
gently played, but the next **C** is arsic and most expressive, as
is the next **A** leading into the final note, similar to the opening anacrusis. If the executant feels the true character of a
long melodic note in this manner, it can never sound dull or
monotonous.

    In the following passage for trumpet and horn from
Schumann's *Symphony No. 1,* the normal note group is
composed of quarters, except for the *dotted quarter-note,*

which must be thought of in terms of eighths (the smallest note-value) in order to properly place (melodically and rhythmically)[17] the eighth that follows it.

EXAMPLE 40

Since the above passage is played moderately, four beats to the measure, the grouping should be as illustrated at (1). The preceding imaginary arsis (in parenthesis) for the first eighth is shown at (2), and should be felt, mentally (in the smaller note group), in order to give character to the up-beat eighth! This note, however, is grouped in accordance with the quarter-note grouping (3), since the beat is in quarter-note values. The thesis *before* the second eighth (in the melody) is the dot after the first quarter (4), so it must be grouped with the larger group (5) of which it is a part. The thesis *following* the second eighth (the second eighth of the smaller group (6) and to which the second eighth in the melody leads) is the first eighth in the *next* quarter-note, so that the second eighth (in the melody) is properly grouped with the quarter (7), and leads into it. The remaining quarters are, of course, grouped in the regular way.

17. Since all the notes in the first measure are on the same line of the staff, the term "rhythmically" applies here. The application of *melodic* principles gives life to the *rhythm* and makes it more exact.

Schumann's *Träumerei* presents several interesting problems:

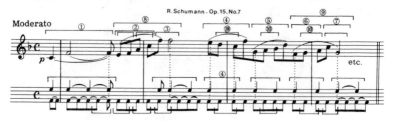

EXAMPLE 41

Here the component values in each note group vary from quarters to eighths. The first group (1) is of quarters, while the second (2) and third (3) are built of eighths. Groups (4), (5), and (6) must be composed of quarters, since they correspond with Schumann's slurs.[18] The middle group of eighths (10) in each of these three larger groups can nevertheless be brought out with great expressive effect. The last group (7) may be played very poignantly if it is perfectly conceived, with the **C** opening the group and *leading* into the **G** with a feeling of finality! In performance, groups (2) and (3) should be mentally combined to form group (8), while groups (6) and (7) should be combined to form group (9). But the small groups are still *felt* within the large ones.

To those readers who may criticize this detailed analysis in the belief that it destroys the spontaneity of the music, the author can only state that only after much analysis does one really know what takes place within a phrase; and the artist that is forearmed with this knowledge has a conviction to his playing or singing that can be obtained in no other way. In the final execution of the music before the public—in the

18. The author does not presume here to criticize the compositions of Schumann. It is well-known that many composers of piano music have differed in their conception and use of the slur sign. Consequently many passages that appear to be slurred are really only *phrased*. In this case the slur signs appear to be legitimate. In any case, slurs on the piano are more imagined than real!

concert performance—should not the quality of the impression made on the audience be the deciding factor? The author has used the above concepts many years, both in the rehearsing of groups and in the teaching of individuals, with much success. The thrill that a teacher feels when a student first grasps the true *musical* sense of the progression of the music through the understanding of the proper note groups, and becomes enthusiastic about it, will not soon be forgotten.

Ternary Rhythm
     As the final part of this section several phrases in ternary rhythm are quoted. First, the same fragment from *L'Apprenti Sorcier* is again examined:

EXAMPLE 42

     As first illustrated in *Ex. 31* **(b)**, (page 66), the grouping in the above example is first in eighths ($\overline{\text{AAT}}$), shown at (1), and then in dotted-quarters (2); the first *measure* being thetic and the second and third arsic. Obviously, this theme was actually conceived in $\frac{9}{8}$ time (3) instead of $\frac{3}{8}$. For this reason every eighth *after* the initial one (in each measure of $\frac{9}{8}$ time (may, in the broadest sense, be considered arsic, leading to the next thesis on the first of the next measure (4). By keeping this in mind the player can give solidity and authority to his phrasing. He should by all means mentally count the three eighths in each of the first two measures (5), even though they are not written, in order to give character to the quarters, and to insure that the three eighths in measure three (6) will be rhyth-

mically perfect. The upbeat (7) should be mentally present
since this is the true arsis and corresponds to the conductor's
preparatory beat. (These three eighth-notes actually do appear later in the recapitulation!)

Next, the *Loin du Bal* by Gillet, a simple little waltz that
contains a valuable lesson in expressive interpretation:

EXAMPLE 43

In the first measure (1) the repeated notes pose a problem
for the student. By grouping them properly however, the difficulty is immediately overcome. As shown in the rhythmic
schematic, the last five eighths of the measure constitute a
large arsis leading to the next thesis (3), especially when played up to tempo (one beat per measure). Instead of mechanically playing these six first eighths in one swoop and accenting the first note, the sensitive artist will start on the first
thesis with only a slight touch, and as the remaining arsic
eighths (2) take their places in the rhythmic scheme there will
be a very slight *crescendo or intensification* up to the thesis,
as shown by the arrows. The thesis, however, is *not* accented! This crescendo should not be consciously made, but
should appear solely as a result of the notes being properly
grouped and felt. Scherchen's "crescendo of intensity" surely applies here also.[19]

In the third excerpt, a quotation from the opera *Carmen,*
Bizet illustrates how perfectly words may be set to music.
The anacrusis in each case is beautifully accentuated through

19. Scherchen, *op. cit.*

the coincidence of the beginning word of each phrase of the
text with the arsis of the musical group!

EXAMPLE 44

In the first measure the word *dis* should be mentally subdivided into note groups of eighths (1) so that the following
eighths can be grouped properly in the most musical manner.
At (2) the larger grouping of dotted-quarters should be used
as shown in the rhythmic schematic. Within this larger conception the smaller groups should also be felt, as at (3), to
more perfectly feel the progression of the melody. If this
quotation is dissected further, one may observe how delicately the note groups fit the intensity of the syllables of the
French words. *Pou, hé, ré,* and *beau* all fall on the strongest
(second) arsis (of the two) in the group. The attention of the
reader is especially called to the fact that the arsis closest to
the barline is always the most intense. More of this shall be
said later.

Mais (English: "but") falls on the first note of the larger
group as well as on a chromaticism, which is as active
musically as is the conjunction in prose or poetry. *Je*
("I"—the most important word in any language!) is always
expressively placed on an arsis, and on the only **sf** in the
passage. At (4), although the principal grouping is in dotted-
quarters, the *je* is still very active (⌐AAT⌐). If the singer should
be in doubt as to where to breathe, she has only to remember

that she must *not* break a group unless the text (5) demands it (the syllable *ponds* cannot be broken, so the felt group is ⌜A̅T̅⌝ [*de moi*], instead of ⌜A̅A̅T̅⌝!), but should breathe *between* groups or combinations of groups, thereby phrasing perfectly.

5 MUSICAL PHENOMENA HIGHLIGHTED BY NOTE GROUPING

In addition to enhancing the expressive qualities of music, note grouping sensitizes or highlights certain rhythmic or melodic phenomena that importantly affect the enjoyment of the listener.

Absence of an Arsis

To quote from the most lyrical of operas, *Faust*, the charm of the rhythmic lilt in the first phrase of the waltz is due to the absence of the normal arsis on the second beat (1). This intensifies the arsis on the third beat (2), and creates a syncopated effect that is intriguing to the ear of the auditor.

EXAMPLE 45

How perfectly this music conforms to the note group units! The *absence of the thesis* as a result of the tie gives prominence to the arsic quality of the dotted-quarters, and the accent which one customarily gives to a syncopation is easily made without it being indicated or over-emphasized.

Absence of a Thesis

In a later phrase of the same waltz, the absence of a thetic pulse in measures two and four (1) due to the ties, gives a light, ethereal quality to the music, since the melody is composed largely of motion-creating (arsic) elements. The arsic eighth-rest (2) also gives importance to the after-beat quarters (3) in the accompaniment (as does the quarter-rest in *Ex. 45*). This eighth-rest also emphasizes the next eighth due again to the absence of a thesis!

EXAMPLE 46

In another short passage from *Carmen,* the absence of a thesis (again the result of a tie) is very effective at (1), giving a beautiful swing to the music coupled with the unexpected absence of a thesis following the arsis *yeux,* and the last syllable, *e,* of *fu-mé-e* (2). Both of these absences make the two arses, *La,* more expressive, musically, because of the natural stress given the article by the use of a rest instead of a note on the theses. Observe again how the text is wedded perfectly to the note groups!

EXAMPLE 47

Increase of Arsic Motion Toward the Barline

As we have shown in the first melody from *Carmen (Ex. 44),* the closer the arsis is to the thesis in the next measure, the more intense the "arsic" feeling; or in other words, the closer the arsis is to the barline, the stronger the *consciousness* of the progression from arsis to thesis (See *Ex. 43,* p. 76). This effect can be observed in the many waltzes in which the third beat is *accented*. A familiar example is the first phrase of the well-known *Blue Danube Waltz* by Johann Strauss:

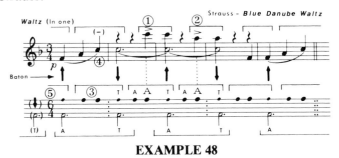

EXAMPLE 48

This third beat accent is one of the characteristic features of the Viennese waltz style. It is the great increase of motion created by this accentuation of the arsis closest to the thesis that makes this style so emotionally effective and stimulating. In the schematic (*Ex. 48*) the *size* of the quarter-notes have been gradually increased in each measure (3) to show the increasing importance of the arses as they approach the barline. (This schematic is obviously *only for illustration* of a concept and should not be taken literally!)

As in all waltzes, the meter is actually $\frac{6}{4}$ (5) (See schematic), the first measure of $\frac{3}{4}$ time being arsic, the second, thetic, and so forth. Therefore the second accent (in the arsic measure) (2) is relatively more important than the first accent (in the thetic measure) (1). The above analysis also explains the slight *tenuto* (4) given to the third quarter in the first measure by some conductors. This is merely recognition of the potency of the last arsis in the measure as an emotional factor in the melody!

The same buildup in emotional content toward the last of the measure may also be observed in $\frac{4}{4}$ time. The first theme in the "Prelude to Act I" of *Die Meistersinger von Nürnberg*

illustrates how Wagner used the potency of the fourth beat to
advantage:

EXAMPLE 49

The schematic shows the increase in arsic feeling toward
the barline. All the smaller, faster-moving notes ((2) in *Ex.
50*) have been placed just before the barline, and this is
shown still more convincingly later on in the composition
when Wagner combines the two principal themes:

EXAMPLE 50

Here the arsic or "moving" notes are placed toward the
end of the measure in *both* melodies. This procedure, plus a
series of eighth-notes in a rhythmic accompanying figure (1),
creates a pulsing, animated, unforgettable passage. Again
the tied eighths (theses) in the bass (3) give added movement
to the arsic eighths.

Accidentals

In writing of the beginnings of musical composition as we
know it today, Ferguson states that when early composers
began to combine melodies containing diverse rhythms, it
was no longer possible to maintain the prevailing custom of
exclusive concord. If any real freedom in their writing was to
be achieved, some discord had to be admitted. He continues:

> Yet neither theorist nor composer could find a wholly
> satisfactory formula for the relation of discord and con-

cord. Both agreed however, that concord must appear on what we should call the strong beat of the rhythm, and that discord might appear on the weak. That such discords were tolerated rather than enjoyed is indicated in the usual defense—that after discord, concord sounds more sweet.[1]

It is clear that centuries ago musicians agreed that *consonance* was a characteristic of the *thesis* and *dissonance* a feature of the *arsis*. The composer, Saint-Saëns, in a lecture on the execution of music, said "expression was introduced into music by the dominant-seventh chord . . ." and that it "has been the open door to all dissonances and the domain of expression. It was a death blow to the learned music of the sixteenth century; it was the arrival of the reign of melody . . ."[2]

As every musician knows, the dominant-seventh chord, or for that matter any dissonance, must normally be resolved,[3] since every action must be followed by rest; dissonances, or "active" intervals, usually resolving to consonances, or "rest" intervals. Also from earliest times, as pointed out, it has been the nature of Western music for dissonance to occur usually on the weak beat, or weak *part* of the beat, and resolve to consonance which occurs on the strong beat, or strong *part* of the beat. These phenomena are completely in accord with the views previously stated. What could be more natural than for the *active* (dissonant) harmony to coincide with the arsis or *motion-creating* part of the beat or measure?

As a result of this coincidence, the greater number of *accidentals* occur on the arses, as a few minutes of study will confirm, since accidentals most often appear as component

1. Donald N. Ferguson, *A History of Musical Thought* (New York: Appleton-Century-Crofts, Inc., 1948), pp. 75-76.
2. Camille Saint-Saëns, *On the Execution of Music and Principally of Ancient Music* (San Francisco: Blair-Murdock Co., 1915), p. 5.
3. While the principles of expression as set forth in this book are based on the structure of conventional harmony, these note-grouping concepts are applicable to all types of musical composition, since the procedures of execution are the same.

parts of actual or implied active harmonic structures. These
accidentals therefore should be given special attention in execution, for in addition to their natural arsic quality, they
have an active harmonic function (modulation) which increases their melodic significance. The following theme from
the music of Moritz Moszkowski illustrates this point:

EXAMPLE 51

In the above melody, each accidental occurs on an arsis
(or on the first note of a group ⌐AT⌐). Therefore note grouping is most helpful in bringing to the attention of the player
the importance of the chromaticisms, or color creating
elements; and consequently the importance of the harmonic
changes in the music. This underscoring of the unusual
elements of the melody intensifies the variety and freshness
of the piece and enhances the expression.

Closer examination of this theme shows that the two
D-sharps at (1) have, in addition to their motive importance
as arses, a strong melodic tendency in each case to return to
the next note, **E;** and the **D-natural** at (2) is made more striking because of the two previous **D-sharps.** Proper use of the
note-grouping method will give these pithy elements of the
music the correct amount of expressive vigor. While the
B-flat at (3) normally receives additional accent due to its being a syncopation, the knowledge of the fact that it is the last
arsis before the barline gives it still more importance musically. It should be apparent that the above principles also apply
to the last four measures of that phrase.

The above instances are only a few of the unlimited
number of delightful musical phenomena resulting from the
delicate use of note grouping in phrasing and interpretation.
In the next chapter more excerpts will be given, with special
emphasis on the use of the note-grouping method in pedagogy.

6 APPLICATION AND USE OF NOTE GROUPING

Pedagogy and Performance

In his excellent book, *Musical Interpretation*, Tobias Matthay writes:

> No one (not even a child beginner) should be allowed to sound any succession of sounds, however simple, without being made clearly to understand that there must be *some* shape or progression even in such primitive attempts; thus:

EXAMPLE 52

even therefore, suggesting harmonies: I-V-I.[1]

Matthay's logic is stimulating and perfectly fits the conception of note grouping as set forth in this text. Another excerpt from the same work is also pertinent:

> It is non-perception of the fact of *progression* that results in all the rhythmical "sloppiness" in playing

1. Tobias Matthay, *Musical Interpretation* (London: Joseph Williams, 1914), p. 45.

passage work [on the piano]. How often we find the poor teacher's pupils playing ♫♫ ; ♫♫ ; instead of ♫♫♫ ♫♫♫ ♪, etc., and ♫♫♫ ; ♫♫♫ ; instead of ♫♫♫♫ ♫♫♫♫ ♫♫♫♫ ♪ , etc.

The pupil should realize that the triplets or quadruplets do not finish with the beginning of the sound of the last note, but, on the contrary, that the group lasts up *to the beginning* of the first note of the *next group.*[2]

Interpreted in the light of the theories presented in Chapter 3, what Matthay is saying is that instead of playing the *patterns* (thesis-arsis) of notes as printed: ♫♫ ♫♫ , or ♫♫♫ ♫♫♫ , the pupil should play the *note groups:* ♫♫ ♫♫ ♪ , *or* ♫♫♫ ♫♫♫ ♪ .

The late William Kincaid, solo flutist *extraordinaire* of the Philadelphia Orchestra for many years, who taught at the Curtis Institute of Music, used to say: "One cannot play a triplet properly in three notes, one must always have *four* notes." For example: ♫♫ ♪ or 1-231-231, etc., not: ♫♫ ♫♫ or 123-123-123, etc. There must be a point of rest before the triplet can sound complete and plausible. No group or phrase comes to its end on a rest! It must end on a note!

"Likewise in quadruplets," he said, "one must have *five* notes: ♫♫♫ ♪ or 1-2341-2341-2341, etc., not: ♫♫♫ ♫♫♫ or 1234-1234-1234, etc."

The question, then, that the teacher must answer is: How may I quickly and easily teach the note-grouping concept to my students so that it can help them to execute whatever they play with musicianship and expression?

2. Matthay, *Ibid.*

Teaching the Method

In order to acquaint the student with note groups and teach him to suppress the playing of printed patterns, it has been found advantageous to indicate each group by means of brackets, marked on the music in pencil, *above the notes,* similar to those in the examples previously shown. The student should then play the music, *one group at a time,* with a short rest between each group, and with the speed of the notes within each group in the *exact tempo* of the piece; thinking of each group as a *separate, coherent unit,* with every *initial* arsis progressing (moving) to the following thesis. It is very important too, that the student have a *mental image of motion* in each group as the arsis moves to the thesis. Only after the phrase has been well played, group by group, each *slightly separated,* should it be played completely through without separation of groups.

The author recommends that the student's first introduction to note grouping be made through the medium of technical exercises (scales, arpeggios, vocalises, etc.), because, of all his music, these studies are usually played the most mechanically. They are also the simplest as far as melodic content is concerned. In the scale of **C** major, for instance, the smallest note groups possible should first be bracketed (without the letters AT if desired, to save time) in this manner:

EXAMPLE 53

The student should then be asked to play this scale very slowly,[3] one group at a time, as a separate unit, thinking of each unit as he plays it as a small, separate entity of the entire passage, such as a syllable of a word (e.g., ⌐Con⌐-⌐stan⌐-⌐ti⌐-⌐no⌐-⌐ple⌐!). Notice how the consonant at the beginning of each syl-

---

3. It is of course obvious by now that only in a very slow tempo can music be thought of in the smallest possible group.

lable is emphasized in speech the way the arsis is stressed in the note group—almost sub-consciously. One teaches reading this way in groups of *letters*—phonetically; why not music in groups of notes? It would be unthinkable to emphasize the *end* of each syllable!

The effect of the arsis being *first* in the group should naturally make it slightly more important in the student's mind, and should cause him to play the group with an *almost imperceptible* increase of tone on the first note, especially in the beginning of note-grouping study. If increase of TONE could be thought of as an increase in the SIZE of the note, this effect could be diagrammed thus:

EXAMPLE 54

and played: 1̄ - 2̄3̄ - 4̄1̄ - 2̄3̄ - 4̄1̄, etc.; the *hyphen* (or in the music, the cutoff sign: //) indicating a slight rest between groups.

It is important that the teacher realize that it is impossible to show in a diagram the *slight amount* of increased sound made by the difference in mental image of the groups—that is, arsis-thesis (note group) instead of thesis-arsis (pattern); and he must *not* permit the student to *accent* the beginning note of the group. If he will say to the student: "Make the first note (arsis) of the group *lead* to the second," he will usually succeed in achieving the proper ratio of dynamics between the two. *Descrescendo* signs are shown in the example (*Ex. 54*) to give the student an *idea* of the way the groups are played dynamically; *however these signs are not to be taken literally!* It must be stressed again that there is a very delicate and almost imperceptible line between artistic expression and ridiculous over-accentuation, wherever that accentuation occurs.

It is remarkable that the accent customarily given to the first note of the printed *pattern* is accepted as proper by so

many (i.e., ♩♩♩♩ ♩♩♩♩), and at the same time is not
recognized as being non-musical. Transfer of this emphasis
to the first note of the *group* for *instructional purposes
only* should not offend even the most sincere purist (i.e.,
♩♩♩♩ ♩♩♩♩ ♪)!

An illustration that aptly conveys to the student the importance of *not exaggerating* the note groups is to compare
their use to an actor's makeup: No "makeup" whatever (no
note grouping—playing patterns) would result in a "pale"
and uninteresting performance; too much "makeup" (over-
emphasis of the note groups) would *sound* the way "Jo Jo"
the clown *looks;* but the artistic and judicious use of coloring
in the makeup of a beautiful actress could be likened to the
correct and musical use of note groups; both giving aesthetic
pleasure to the audience.

After each group is properly felt and understood, and
can be played group by group with precision, the student
should combine the smaller groups, two by two, into larger
ones, which should then be marked as follows:

EXAMPLE 55

and played: 1 - 2341 - 2341 - 2341, etc. or:

EXAMPLE 56

There will naturally be an *increase in tempo* as the smaller
groups are combined into larger ones, for the first grouping
(*Ex. 53*) is beaten in subdivided four, or in eight beats to the
measure (one eighth-note to a beat), while the second (*Ex.
55*) is played in four beats to the measure.

In a still faster tempo, two of the larger groups are combined, making eight sixteenth-notes in each group, which are played in $\frac{2}{2}$ time or *alla breve* (¢). These groups should be marked:

EXAMPLE 57

and played:

EXAMPLE 58

The above is to be executed separately; first in groups, to get the sweep of the group (in two); and then together with no break, giving a lightness to the run!

In arpeggios, chords, etc., the same principles apply. An arpeggio, for instance, in **C** major played *allegro,* four beats per measure should be marked:

EXAMPLE 59

and first played:

EXAMPLE 60

After the performance of each group is fluent, groups are combined as in *Ex. 59.*

All of the above samples should at first be practiced *very slowly* in separate groups. The student may then gradually quicken the tempo, as the feeling for the note groups develops, until the next larger group is reached. After he has a thorough grasp of the note-grouping principle, and can feel the progression of the music in groups, *from the smallest to the largest,* he may be permitted to combine the larger groups into sections and phrases.

This method of approach should always be used when the student is first given a new exercise or piece, for it is of the utmost importance that the initial impression be one of *groups* and not of printed *patterns!* He must learn to *look* at the music *differently than it is printed!* In fact he reads *on* the beat but plays *off* the beat! *From up to down!* By studying the exercise in this way he will avoid mechanical playing and will learn to *make MUSIC* of even a simple scale. (Although as any accomplished musician knows, it is never easy to play even the simplest of scales.)

In beginning the study of a composition, for example, the melody of the first theme of the last movement of Beethoven's *Third Concerto* for piano and orchestra:

EXAMPLE 61

should be practiced first as it is shown in *Ex. 62,* then as in *Ex. 63,* and then as in *Ex. 64.*

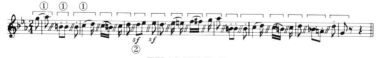

EXAMPLE 62

As each group is practiced, the *articulations* and *accents* as written should always be observed, as shown in (1) in *Ex. 62* (above); for in using note grouping, the expression marks of the music are *not affected* in any way. All signs of interpretation (slurs, *staccato* or *tenuto* marks, *ritardandos,* etc.) should be scrupulously observed; the note groups being only superimposed, *mentally,* over the composer's dynamic, rhythmic, and expressive indications. Notice particularly at (2), how Beethoven put the *sf*'s over the arses and not the theses!

While each group is being played, to again reinforce this point, the first note of the group should be *thought of* as being more important, only for the reason that it is *first* in the group *one is looking at;* also the first note should be conceived as *leading* to the second. While at first it may seem to the reader that there is little practicality in recommending so much "thinking" and "feeling" of the note groups, instead of simply telling the student to accent the arsis and slight the thesis; but it must be remembered that the difference between the performance of an excellent technician and that of an artist is an aesthetic and interpretative one. A difference that cannot be arrived at by following such simple directions.

An artistic interpretation in reality is created more by the artist's *mental conception* of the work (provided he is faithful to the inherent musical qualities of the composition) than by any *technical* devices that he uses. Any procedure that would interfere in any way with the composer's written wishes as shown in the music—such as accenting a note— would be foreign to the ethics of any musician of integrity. In this, every performing artist should be a *purist!*

The proper use of note grouping does *not* change the music. Everything the composer has expressed on the printed page must be re-created, insofar as humanly possible, exactly as shown thereon. Note grouping does, however, if utilized correctly, bring out intrinsic, inspirational qualities that *cannot be written,* and assist the performer to conceive the work he is playing or singing in a more artistic, moving and *musical* manner. Such a conception of the composition can result only in a more inspired and aesthetically satisfying performance. If the repetition of the author's recommendations for using the note-grouping approach appears redundant at times, it can only be justified as reinforcement. Old habits are not changed easily and some reiteration seems valid due to the many ramifications of applying these concepts.

After the melody has been thoroughly practiced by the student in small groups it should then be played using the *next larger groups,* which in this excerpt correspond to the actual tempo of the music but which are still played separately (two beats to the measure):

EXAMPLE 63

As shown at (1), the note groups coincide with the quarter-note rhythm and grouping (shown in the schematic in *Ex. 61*) when played at this tempo.[4]

When the student is able to play each of these larger groups with expression, making a very slight decrescendo[5] from the beginning to the end of each group (recognizing that each is composed of two smaller groups), he may then play the whole melody; mentally adding two of the above groups to make a section, four to make a phrase, and so forth, as shown here:

EXAMPLE 64

4. See *Ex. 28,* p. 64.

5. This remark may seem paradoxical in view of the discussion presented in Chapter 4 concerning progression toward the barline, however the *tempo* is the determining factor. In the melody from *Die Meistersinger,* the progression of the meter in *four* beats to the measure created the increase in motion toward the barline; but since *this* melody is in *two* beats to the measure, each group is more unified, and the entire anacrusis should be thought of as a *whole,* leading to the next thesis across the barline.

It is interesting to analyze briefly several of the musical aspects of the above melody that are highlighted through the use of note grouping. The three **B-naturals** in the first measure (1), instead of being mechanically repeated, take on new character, in that the first leads to the second in the smaller group, and the third progresses to the **C** in the next measure, the two smaller groups giving life and meaning to their repetition, and preventing the monotony that always plagues repeated notes on the same line or space on the staff. Then the two small groups are combined, making an animated succession leading to the thesis.

The **D** in the second measure (2), being the end of a group and a tiny thesis, stands almost by itself and is just touched, giving expression through contrast to the three sixteenths that follow it.[6] The same analysis holds true for the **A-flat** (3) in the fifth measure. If it is played as the end of the group it will have a light, delicate character that will delight the listener. The **B-flat** (4) in the seventh measure, being the first of its group, is musically important for it creates variety with the preceding **B-natural** in measure five, as well as being the note by which the melody modulates into the dominant minor key (**G-minor**). Note also that the chromatic run in measure four (5), occurs on the last half of the measure (or the arsis, in *quarter-note* groups), and is most effective for this reason.

In practicing the Alberti bass in the left hand (*Ex. 61 (1)*), the student should first play the groups from the smallest to the largest as outlined in the foregoing paragraphs. If properly done, this will not only give increased movement to the passage, but will also lend slightly more tone to the repeated **G**'s than to the lower bass notes. As the author has repeatedly pointed out, note grouping is a *melodic* phenomenon, and, strictly speaking, does not apply to this pedal **G** which is *harmonic* in nature. Therefore to compensate for the slight in-

---

6. After this idea is clearly understood, the entire upbeat pattern of sixteenth-notes may be grouped together as a complete arsis in quarter-note meter (*Ex. 61 (2)* and *(3)*, p. 91). One should always be conscious however of the small groups (*Ex. 61 (4)*) existing within the larger group, again subtly noting especially the chromaticisms.

crease of tone in the upper portion, the *lower* notes must be grouped as if they were alone in the measure as simple eighth-notes, as follows:

EXAMPLE 65

This will give even more motion and expressiveness to the bass by treating it as another melody and by giving the *harmonic* changes *melodic* significance. At first the piano student should practice note grouping in each hand separately and then combine hands. In the beginning this will be difficult for most students (grouping notes in each hand simultaneously); however one only has to listen to any premier concert pianist to hear that it is always done! (See *Appendix A.*) *Learning to hear* note grouping with a discerning ear is the first step to being convinced of its value and its universal use by the foremost performers.

When the whole is combined in the manner recommended above and the student has observed all of the written directions of the composer, the result is a scintillating, moving, and expressive theme of Beethoven!

Special Applications

In teaching *voice*, note grouping will enable the instructor and consequently the student to know instinctively where to breathe—*musically* speaking. Of course if the *text* forbids a breath between note groups, an earlier or later spot must be chosen; however if the prosody is excellent the composer will have fitted the music so perfectly to the words that the singer will have no difficulty in this regard.

The operas of Verdi are excellent examples of the perfect wedding of music to words. (See *Exs. 44* and *47.*) There is never any question as to the correct breathing place, and the note-groups are easily apparent throughout. Verdi, like most of the great composers, seemed to have had a predilection for the upbeat. He undoubtedly understood and felt its tremen-

dous power of expression. In the tragic final scene of his
opera *Aïda,* one of the most moving passages in all operatic
literature (a duet between two dying lovers), Verdi has taken
pains to mark the arsis (in quarter-note grouping) with an accent, so the singer will stress this particular upbeat; thereby
giving tension and dramatic import to both the music and
words.

O ter-ra ad-di-o; ad-di-o val-le di pian-ti.— So-gno di gau-dio che in do-lor __ sva-ni

EXAMPLE 66

In actual practice, the accented notes are usually *held* by
the singer (Verdi has even marked the second one *tenuto*),
giving additional emphasis to the poignant qualities of the
melody. While the smaller groups are important, the composer has thus indicated that here the *quarter-note groups*
should be given the most importance:

EXAMPLE 67

His compositional mood was no doubt influenced by the
type of accompaniment he desired; four simple chords per
measure, each occurring *on* the beat:

EXAMPLE 68

It is clear that even though the melody moves in eighth-
notes, the underlying note groups in quarter-notes must be

mentally present if the passage is to be sung correctly! In other words, if one is *thinking* in quarter-notes in ♯ meter, the quarter note arses (beats 2 and 4) are felt: [musical notation] ; however if one is thinking in eighths, then the second eighth of each beat is important: [musical notation] . Again the tempo will determine which is used.

Many more passages could be quoted; however if the singer will only let note grouping come to his aid, seldom will he breathe in the wrong place, and the inner, expressive arses will give a quiet energy and vigor to his song.

The *wind player* has many of the same problems in performance as the singer. There is always the same question of where to breathe and how much breath should be taken for each particular phrase. Since he doesn't have any text to worry him, the wind instrumentalist should assiduously apply note grouping to his playing at all times. By so doing he will immediately solve most of his phrasing problems.

If singers (when the text permits) and wind players will always breathe *between groups* (therefore seldom breathe at the barline!), the phrases and periods will be easy to see and to play, and the same comparable and satisfying musical results will be forthcoming from the use of note grouping that were shown to be possible on the piano (Study *Exs. 61, 62, 62,* and *64).*

String players also are helped to play musically and to phrase correctly by the use of the note-grouping concept. The pedagogy is almost the same as the foregoing with the exception of bowing. Normally one usually thinks of an *upbeat* as meaning that an *upbow* must be used, but the former conductor of the National Symphony in Washington, D.C., Howard Mitchell, said that many times he instructed the string section of his orchestra to use a *downbow* on an *upbeat* to stress the anacrusis, as well as to de-emphasize the thesis. He recommended for example that in the *Eine Kleine Nachtmusik* of Mozart, the opening anacrusis in the last

movement be played with a downbow to give it life, and to
prevent an accented downbeat.

EXAMPLE 69

Mitchell, an excellent 'cellist, also said that in fast passages where the strings have two equal sixteenth-notes slurred, it is sometimes difficult to obtain proper articulation of
the second sixteenth-note [in the printed pattern]. For instance, in the following excerpt from Beethoven's *Eroica
Symphony,* violinists usually stress the first sixteenth of each
small pattern and ignore the importance of the second!

EXAMPLE 70

It is obvious here that if the player were to use the note-
grouping principle this difficulty would disappear. He would
then mentally conceive of the two sixteenth-notes, not as
♩♩ ♩♩ ♪ , but as ♩ ♩♩ ♩♩♪ ; so that the second sixteenth would be accorded slightly more arsic importance,
and be grouped with the eighth-note following it. In this way
the passage acquires clearness, evenness and precision.

The Rôle of the Barline

If true melody is devoid of "thumping" meter, it follows
that in some types of expressively played melodies the position of the barline should not be easily recognizable to the
auditor. This is especially true of the music of the impres-
sionistic school. In Claude Debussy's *L'Après-midi d'un
Faune,* for instance, the flute solo should be almost devoid of
metric rhythm in the strictest sense, and when properly inter-

preted should give the listener a completely "beat-free" impression.

Also in descriptive pieces, such as the *Flight of the Bumble Bee* by Rimsky-Korsakow, the musical effect is most gratifying if the rhythm is confined to the eighth-note accompaniment in the strings, and the flute be permitted to play quite freely without giving an impression that a barline exists. This may be easily accomplished if the player groups the notes properly and avoids any rhythmic accent of the printed patterns.

Émile Stiévenard writes the following paragraph which eloquently states the solution of the barline problem:

> Modern musicians recognize that the usefulness of the barline has been poorly understood for two centuries and that theorists have attributed to it a function that it doesn't possess. The measure is only the mechanical means for executing with precision the duration of the notes that succeed each other in the music.[7]

He continues to say that the barline is a purely conventional sign that does not enter at all into the musical design itself; its use being analogous to the white lines that divide a school book—it guides the reader, nothing more. The executant needs only the *rythme,* or phrase of the melody itself. For thousands of years, he reminds us, we have made music without barlines but not without measured phrases, because melody can only have form and sense if it is measured.[8]

Later in his book he gives us a sentence that contains the essence of the discussion: "In reality, measures haven't in themselves any relation with musical feeling."[9] This pursues the same line of reasoning that we have used all along. If the executant will endeavor to *forget the barline* except as a means for insuring the correct meter, or the exact duration of the notes in the music he is playing, he will avoid the habit of making the listener monotonously feel the position of these

7. Stiévenard, *op. cit.,* p. 18.
8. *Ibid.*
9. *Ibid.,* p. 22.

vertical "trouble makers," and the *music itself* will be all that
he hears!

Rhythmic Figures

There is another way in which note grouping can aid the
performer. This consists of helping him to correctly execute
certain important rhythmic problems in the music. It is gen-
erally recognized that there are a few combinations of note-
values that are difficult to teach students to play correctly
with "musicianship." These same figures are also trying for
the performing artist, regardless of his technical mastery,
and he must always devote his attention to these elusive combinations of notes if the music is to be interpreted correctly
with style.

One of the most difficult of these is the *dotted-eighth and
sixteenth-note* figure: ♪♪♪♪ , etc. (or as it *should* be
called: *sixteenth and dotted-eighth!*). This rhythm is pecu-
liarly troublesome to play correctly. At a fast tempo, technical problems (fingering, register, etc.) usually arise to worry
the performer, and the result is all too often: ♪♪♪♪ .
If the student will assiduously practice the figure *one group
at a time:* ♪♪ ♪♪ ♪♪ ♪♪ , etc., slightly emphasizing the sixteenth, he will gradually achieve mastery of this enigma.
Each single group should be played quickly—that is, with the
two notes as close together as possible. After this has been
done he may combine groups until the whole is played correctly.

One method successfully used by the author in teaching
this rhythm is as follows: First, *sing* each group (♪♪) separately (singing Ta-Ta), and have the student immediately afterward play the same figure, imitating the teacher by rote. Second, sing two or more groups together (♪♪ ♪♪ or Ta-Ta Ta-Ta ,
etc.), the student playing immediately afterward. Third, continue until the student has the rhythm under control. It may

take several weeks or even months to master this difficult rhythm.

In *fast* music one *never plays* (holds) *the dot:* ♪♩. ♪♩., etc., but should play the dotted-eighth *short:* ♩♪♪♩♪♪ , or as written: ♩♪♩♪♩♪♩ . At a *slower* tempo it is still more difficult to play this figure with musicianship. To cite another work of Beethoven, the second movement of the *Violin Concerto in D Major* opens with the following motive in the strings, which is later imitated by other instruments of the orchestra:

EXAMPLE 71

At this tempo it is not easy to keep the above motive from sounding: ♩♪♪. If the note grouping principle is used however, the problem is much simpler: ♩♪♪. If the performer will keep in mind that the sixteenth must progress to the next quarter, the correct musical feeling will be attained. Here the dot *is* played and the sixteenth *lengthened* because of the slower tempo.

This same figure causes even more trouble when it occurs in ⅜ time: ⅜♩♫♫♫♫♫♫, etc. Here again the groups should first be *sung* and then played separately: ♫♪♫♪♫♪ , etc., and then combined ⅜♩♫♩♫♩♫♩♫♪, etc. Interpretation of the dot in fast music is the same as before: it becomes a sixteenth rest! In the first movement of the *Seventh Symphony*, Beethoven writes a sixteenth-rest instead of a dot for the first few measures to show that in a fast tempo the dot must *not* be held (𝄽 𝄽).

Triplets are also constant offenders in that they are often rushed and are not played their exact value. The reader is referred again to Matthay's observation pertinent to this question which we have previously quoted on page 86, line 3. It must be repeated again that if the student will read the groups: ♪♪♪ ♪♪♪ ♪♪♪ ♪ , etc., instead of reading the patterns: ♪♪♪ ♪♪♪ ♪♪♪ , etc., it will help considerably in correcting this problem.

It is apparent that if note grouping is used, the faulty rhythmic sense that causes the above and other errors of this type can from the beginning be prevented from developing, and the pupil can avoid falling into the bad performance habits that result in this kind of playing. By grouping triplets as in the previous paragraph, and quadruplets: ♫♫♫♫ , etc., it is hardly possible for the performer not to realize that *the note group must not be broken between patterns,* and that music is *not* played one beat or measure at a time.

Ad Libitum Cadenzas

Cadenzas, especially those *ad libitum* ones which have no apparent metric scheme, often present problems in phrasing that perplex the player. If the teacher will group the notes in these bravura passages, arbitrarily selecting those notes which he believes to be truly *arsic* in nature as the *first* ones in each group (using as a guide what would normally be the printed patterns—see *Ex. 72* (1)), the entire cadenza will be much clearer to the student and his audience, and will have plausibility and preciseness. Moreover, once he memorizes the cadenza in this manner (with groups), he will have an additional aid to bolster his memory at the performance.

The following cadenza from Max Bruch's beautiful *Concerto No. 1* for violin, is an excellent example of the above reasoning. It has been grouped in the diagram according to the interpretation of Nathan Milstein (as heard on Columbia LP Record: ML 2003), accompanied by the New York Philharmonic conducted by John Barbirolli.

Bruch - *Violin Concerto No. 1 in G Minor, Op. 26*

Cadenza |Measure 10 | As grouped by Nathan Milstein on Columbia LP Record ML 2003

EXAMPLE 72

At (1) is shown what would be the *normal pattern* if a metric scheme is superimposed on this cadenza. Milstein's groupings follow exactly what would be the *normal note groups* if these notes were written in rhythm. Unfortunately this record is no longer extant.

Two or More Melodies

While the above remarks have been mostly confined to the grouping of single melodies or rhythms, it is obvious that the same principles apply to polyphonic music for the keyboard wherein *two or more* melodies are combined. Each melody should first be grouped individually and practiced alone (hands separate), then combined with the others to form a moving, expressive whole. A measure (*No. 28*) from one of the *Three-part Inventions* by Bach clearly illustrates this procedure:

Bach - *Three-part Invention No. 2.* Measure 28

EXAMPLE 73

The number of applications of note grouping is of course unlimited, and it is obvious that all of them cannot possibly be covered within the space of this book. Suffice it to say that in the hands of an intelligent teacher or performer, note grouping can be an invaluable aid and help in achieving the level of artistic playing or singing that will create pleasure and arouse emotion in the listener.

Recognition

It is imperative however that in the initial stages of learning the method the student be under the constant supervision of an instructor. It is difficult sometimes for a performer to tell when he is properly grouping the notes and when he is wrongly playing patterns. He can therefore easily become discouraged and feel that note grouping is having no effect on his playing. If the performer will be patient, however, he will soon realize the efficacy of the method, particularly when he *learns to recognize its use,* or lack of use, in the playing of other individuals. This recognition of note grouping in all of its subtlety, notably in the playing of great artists, is another of the pleasures of listening to music which this concept will add to the auditory senses, one which will give enjoyment quite as keen as the thrill that comes through actually playing the groups with expression and meaning.

This facet of note grouping will be taken up in the next chapter wherein the playing of several great interpretative artists will be analyzed in the light of the note-grouping theory. In this connection, knowledge of note grouping can be beneficial to the music lover as well as the musician, for it will teach him something else to look for in the playing of the artist, and will give him another standard by which to judge the performance that he hears. After one learns to group notes in his own playing he will *never listen to music in quite the same way* as he did previously.

It has been the author's experience that from six to eight months to several years daily study and practice (depending upon the musical sensitivity of the player) are required before note grouping begins to be an integral part of one's execution, and sometimes even longer. The results are well worth the effort however, and the performer will acquire not only expressive execution, but added technical and musical ability, plus the confidence and assurance that go with system and order in study and analysis. Through many tests and experiments the author has found that the audience *senses* the feeling of professionalism and conviction that the artist conveys when note grouping, in contrast to the mechanical and over-rhythmical feeling listeners have when the player plays only patterns.

Conducting

There are endless ways that note grouping may be used in conducting, for the conductor is a teacher, not only of one performer but of many. All the applications pertinent to the individual instrumentalist may be employed, plus many others that particularly aid in achieving more perfect ensemble playing. It is evident that if note grouping makes a *soloist's* execution more musical, it will, if applied to each member or section in an ensemble, also make the performance of the *entire group* more musical. The conductor therefore should apply the note-grouping principles to each part of the group; achieving thereby a remarkably coherent and stylistic result.

To illustrate, if one takes one measure (*No. 48*) from Haydn's *Symphony No. 101* (The Clock), and group the dif-

ferent melodies in progress simultaneously at that particular
moment, the following result will be obtained:

EXAMPLE 74

While at first glance this procedure appears quite compli-
cated, in reality it is rather simple. If each voice is properly
grouped and played (the same as in *Ex. 73*), the whole will
have a movement and beauty that is indescribable.

In beating time the conductor should at all times be conscious of *power in the upbeat,* and continually stress this fact
to the players or singers. Another quote from Father Finn is
pertinent:

A young conductor is usually advised by veterans to
develop an *authoritative* downbeat. This is good advice in
the beginning; it serves his preliminary need of marking off
the measures carefully and assures the performers of his

control. But, after a very short experience, he should learn that a down beat will take care of itself, by the insistence of a sort of musical [law of] gravity. Having noted this fact, he should address himself to the much more difficult task of indicating the relative lightness [movement] of unaccented notes [arses] and especially of the upbeat.[10]

Later on he writes (almost as if in corroboration of note grouping!): "The unaccented note [arsis] in normal [metric] patterns should have the first consideration of the conductor."[11]

It should be pointed out that the "upbeat" mentioned in the above paragraph should be interpreted as being not only the upswing movement of the baton on the second, third, or fourth beat of the measure, as the meter indicates, but also every smaller arsis *within* those beats. The conductor may also obtain excellent musical results by applying note grouping not only to melodic voices, but also to purely rhythmic and harmonic passages.

In the second movement of the *Seventh Symphony* of Beethoven, the first theme is almost wholly rhythmic and harmonic:

EXAMPLE 75

If the director is not careful this passage will be played with an accent on the first note of each measure, with the result that the two eighths are slighted each time they occur, and the passage loses all feeling of progression. By grouping the second eighth to the quarter as shown at (1), this metrical emphasis can be avoided, and life infused into this somber phrase. Some may argue that this is one theme that has no

10. Finn, *op. cit.,* p. 22.
11. *Ibid.,* p. 23. Here, the author believes *"unaccented note"* means *arsis*.

"understood" upbeat, since the first three sections end on the second beat (arsis). It is for this reason that grouping the quarter-notes at (2) and in succeeding measures is not advised. Beethoven might have felt a lack of preparation in this case, for he placed an opening chord in the woodwinds and horns in the two measures preceding this passage to serve as an introduction! In addition he placed a full quarter-rest before each repetition of the entire phrase (*Ex 75,* (3)).

At this point it is appropriate to remind the reader that there are exceptions to all rules, and note grouping is often modified by the many dynamic and emotional aspects of the music. While the basic sequences of action and repose are *always present,* they are often somewhat suppressed by emotional, accentual and *traditional* aspects of interpretation. Only through years of study, attendance at concerts and listening to recordings—*score in hand*—can the student appreciate to the fullest the true rôle of the arsis in music.

It appears to this author that the more intellectual of the great composers—Bach, Brahms, Wagner, etc.—seem to have written mostly themes beginning with an anacrusis; while the more natural, folk-song oriented composers—Beethoven, Schubert, Schumann, Smetana, to name a few—seem to have preferred many times those themes starting *on* the down-beat (thesis). It is well-known that the themes of much folk-music start on the first beat of the measure, probably due to the influence of the dance.

As one can readily hear, these themes are less active and less thrilling emotionally than those starting with an arsis. Nostalgia plays an important rôle in the love of folk music and emotion here is hard to define. If perhaps the reader does not agree with the preceding paragraphs, at least they are something to think about!

Returning to Beethoven's *Seventh (Ex. 75);* as soon as the counter-melody enters (measure 27 of the movement), the importance of the above theme is relatively reduced, and the listener's attention may then be transferred to the more melodic aspects of the new entry.

Finally, in simple rhythmic figures, such as those found in military marches or in waltzes, note grouping will relieve the monotony of these repetitive notes, and endow them with interest and life. Illustrated below are several measures of the typical "bass and after-beat" accompaniment usually found in parade marches:

EXAMPLE 76

Instead of stolidly and monotonously accenting the first note in each measure, the bass instruments should group the notes as shown at (1). The dominant being active (and an arsis), it should receive a little more attention than the tonic—a rest chord! This uninteresting part will immediately come alive and take on new meaning, and the whole ensemble will benefit musically. The same idea could be applied to the beats of the bass drum! Also the after-beats should be grouped as at (2). By thus giving coherence to these usually uninteresting accompanying figures (providing of course that their dynamic level is always beneath the melody), the march is enriched with motive power and is thrilling to hear. In giving the *harmonic* parts *melodic* significance the movement and animation of the whole is increased. The discerning conductor will find many more instances where note grouping can be of aid, especially if he will always remember those words of Father Finn which we quoted in Chapter 1: *"The mystery of music is in the up-beat."*[12]

12. Finn, *op. cit.*, p. ii.

7 NOTE GROUPING IN THE PLAYING OF GREAT ARTISTS

In order to show that the foremost of today's interpretive artists use the principles of note grouping in their execution to achieve expression and movement, short excerpts from a few representative recordings of important musical works have been selected for illustration and analysis in this chapter; each played by a musician of international renown.

The number of quotations from each work is very limited due to space, and each is shown for only a few measures, but an effort has been made to select passages that show without a doubt that the notes therein have been played in arsis-thesis groups by the performer—either consciously or through the dictates of their innate musicianship and genius—thereby giving aesthetic style to the music.

Two of the recordings selected are not current ones but may be found in reissued form in the collections listed. In addition there are numerous discs that are more current which will prove revealing regarding the degree to which many performers use the arsis-thesis concept, provided the reader *follows the score* while listening and analyses the groups as the artist plays. *(See Appendix A)*. It is hoped that the reader will not stop with the few recordings listed, but will continue to listen for the eloquence in interpreted music resulting from the practice of the arsis-thesis concept. The author is positive the listener will be rewarded with a new appreciation of the intricacies of musical performance and a widened horizon of musical understanding.

Analyses of Recorded Artists

While listening to these and other records, it is recommended that the reader pay particular attention to the following:

(1) The usual avoidance of a thetic emphasis in *very expressive* places in the music, especially at the highest point in the phrase (the way an artist singer begins a high, long tone, for example);

(2) The immediate loss of expression and emotional quality as soon as a rhythmic, bravura passage requires the downbeat to be accented;

(3) The absence of a barline feeling or thetic beat emphasis in runs or fast passages;

(4) The downbeat may occasionally be emphasized for interpretative reasons, but almost invariably the upbeat before it is *just as loud* or *louder*; and

(5) The smaller notes are usually played a bit more prominently than large ones, especially in singing, sustained, cantilena-style melodies.

It is strongly recommended that while playing the recordings the reader first study each short analysis *together with the score*. (The measure numbers are shown.) Otherwise the true significance of these remarks will not be appreciated. Then by following the music of the entire work he will immediately see the groupings as they occur in the rest of the performance.

Analysis I

Johannes Brahms: *Concerto No. 2 in B-Flat Major, Opus 83,* for Piano and Orchestra. Vladimir Horowitz, *Piano,* and the NBC Symphony, Arturo Toscanini, *Conductor.* Victor: DM-740. This recording is no longer available, but has been reissued in RCA Red Seal Album No. CRM4-0914 (A four-record set), *Horowitz, His Complete Recorded Concerto Repertoire.* (Recorded 1940.) This same recording has been used for *Exs. 77-80.*

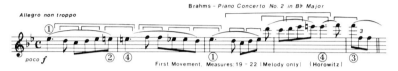

EXAMPLE 77

First movement, *Allegro non troppo.* Measures 19-22.

Definite note grouping for expressive effect. Although Brahms has marked this passage *poco forte,* Horowitz plays the thesis at (1) *piano* in both phrases, probably to avoid a mechanical ictus on the first beat. At (2) there is a slight hesitation to emphasize the heaviness of the arsis before the light thesis. Notice how the complete arsis of the entire measure is played by combining the three smaller ⌐AT⌐ groups to make one larger ⌐AT⌐ group. Horowitz completely ignores the phrase marks (slurs) written by Brahms. At (3) Horowitz plays the **F** in the bass (not shown) *fortissimo* to stress the structural harmony, but observe the lightness of the top melodic note! At (4) the soloist highlights the accidentals foreign to the key to accentuate the variety they create! These are the only accented theses: the ones with the alterations.

EXAMPLE 78

First movement, *Allegro non troppo*. Measures 81-82.

Observe how perfectly Brahms has written this passage to give it life. He divides the triplets ⌐AAT⌐ so there will be no misinterpretation of the note group. Who can construe triplets as ⌐TAA⌐ after hearing this passage? Notice also how Brahms has placed the first note in each figure (group) on the first arsis, and reinforced it with the second (closest to the thesis and the most important!) in the left hand!

Second Movement, Measures: 269-270 [Horowitz]

EXAMPLE 79

Second movement, *Allegro appassionato*. Measures 269-270.

The first **E-flat** is delicately played so the groups will start from the second note (first arsis) of the triplet. This note is ever so lightly stressed to give the passage airiness and motion. The last two notes at (1) are hardly played, since there is no thesis for them to lead to in the next measure. Notice that the slurs are marked contrary to the way the notes are actually grouped by Horowitz. The subtleness of his artistry is demonstrated so beautifully in the way he treats the triplets (⌐AAT⌐)!

Third Movement, Measures: 27- 28 [Melody only] [Horowitz]

EXAMPLE 80

Third movement, *Andante*. Measures 27-28.

The second two measures of this passage have been chosen because they are pitched higher and can be heard better on the record. The groups bring out in relief the separate musical units. Especially is this true of the repeated notes at the end of the second measure. Accents on the first of each pattern would make the triplets sound mechanical. Brahms has tied the first eighth to insure that the first *moving* note is the beginning of a note group (arsis), and this feeling continues throughout the run. (Only the top melodic line has been illustrated in the example.)

Analysis 2

Max Bruch: *Concerto No. 1 in G Minor, Opus 26,* for Violin and Orchestra. Nathan Milstein, *Violin,* and the Philharmonia Orchestra, Leon Barzin, *Conductor.* Angel: 35730.

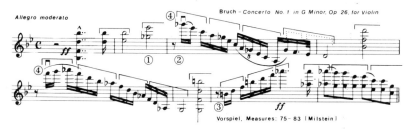

EXAMPLE 81

First movement, *Vorspiel, Allegro moderato.* Measures 75-83.

Note grouping is clearly heard in this excerpt. The second half-note in measure 76, shown at (1), is definitely the first note in a group of two half-notes, but has no thesis to which it can lead. This makes the entrance in the next measure (2) very effective. Notice also at (4) that Bruch marked the beginning of these runs *downbow,* which in effect intensifies the beginning arses, giving brilliance and movement to the music. This passage in sixteenth-notes is convincingly played due to the definiteness of the groups as diagrammed. The rest of the passage is obviously grouped, with measure 81, (3) being exceptionally clear in this regard.

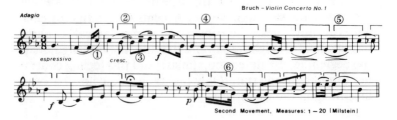

EXAMPLE 82

Second movement, *Adagio*. Measures 1-20.

In this intense and emotional melody, the expressive qualities are exquisitely played. The sixteenth-note that begins the group at (1) is warm and heartfelt. Notice the *diminuendo* toward the end of the group at (2) which gives more expression to the arsis (3). The repeated notes at (4) are even marked *crescendo* by Bruch so there will be no possibility of their being played mechanically. The artist ignores the diminuendo at (5) in order to phrase the group correctly from the arses **D** and **E-flat** to the thesis **C**. The accidental, **C-flat,** is poignantly played as it leads to the next **B-flat**. The soloist purposely breaks the written slurs at (6) in order to preserve the correct note groups. His noble tone is exhibited to the fullest in this moving melody by his exploitation of the musical possibilities in every arsis.

Analysis 3

Georg Philipp Telemann: *Concerto No. 4 in D Major* for Flute and Strings. Jean-Pierre Rampal, *Flute,* and the Saar Radio Chamber Orchestra, Karl Ristenpart, *Conductor.* Columbia: Y 32890.

EXAMPLE 83

First movement, *Andante,* Measures 7-9.
The motion exhibited in the two arsic sixteenths is easily heard. As you listen, note the way Rampal holds the first note of each slurred group and still brings out the second sixteenth (a small arsis), especially at (2) (shown in the dotted bracket). At (1) he lifts off the **A** slightly, due to the skip downward, but at (3) he plays the two slurs without separation (as is customarily done) due to the scalewise movement.

Observe how the artist makes the repeated **G** at (4) come alive as the first note in the group and how he brings out the **G-sharp** at (5) because of its arsic character and its chromatic importance. Follow this entire piece *with the score in hand* and you cannot help but feel the security, control, and musicality the use of note grouping imparts to the interpretation. Regarded by many as the greatest flutist of today, Rampal, with unbelievably beautiful tone, shows artistry and style rarely heard.

The legendary French-American oboist, Marcel Tabuteau, with whom the author studied woodwind ensemble, came from the same background as Rampal, and Tabuteau's use of note grouping can readily be heard in the next example and on the many recordings made by him during the 20s, 30s and 40s as solo oboist with the Philadelphia Orchestra.

Analysis 4

George Friedrick Händel: *Concerto No. 3 in G Minor* for Oboe and String Orchestra. Marcel Tabuteau, *Oboe,* and the Philadelphia Orchestra, Eugene Ormandy, *Conductor. First Chair.* Columbia: ML 4629A. This recording was sold for the benefit of the Philadelphia Orchestra Pension Fund and is no longer extant. It may be obtained from many libraries, however, and should be heard, because in addition to M. Tabuteau, William Kincaid, the former solo flutist of the Philadelphia Orchestra, who also taught note grouping to his students, plays Charles T. Griffes' beautiful *Poem for Flute and Orchestra* on this same disc.

EXAMPLE 84

First movement, *Grave* (♪ = 70) (Subdivided in eight). Measures 6-8.

The incomparable Tabuteau was more than an oboist. He was a master teacher, not only of oboe, but of style and musicianship. His students are legion and his teaching methods have influenced countless players on many different kinds of instruments. He was a firm advocate of note grouping and explained this concept to his students in many different ways.

This short excerpt is only a taste of the beauty he created each time he played. A superior artist, he considered every note to have musical possibilities, and hearing his phrasing and nuances is always a thrilling and emotional experience. In this passage, Tabuteau plays the opening **G** very gently, since it is a thesis with no apparent arsis (the arsis being **F-sharp** in the accompaniment). Immediately the **A** takes on life as the arsis (thinking in eighth-notes), and the thirty-second **G** is brought out (3) as are the two thirty-seconds (4) and all the small arses in the passage. Note the intensification of the dotted-eighth at (3). The note groups throughout this performance can be very clearly heard.

Take particular heed of the way Tabuteau plays the sustained note at (2). Observe the underlying movement of the eighth-notes in the schematic at (1), which causes these sustained notes to take on life and meaning. Being conscious of these subdivisions within the written notes gives them singing quality and exactness. Listen to the minute silence before the two thirty-second notes at (5) and (6). A note attains prominence when it is *preceded* by an instantaneous silence. Again at (2) the "understood" *crescendo* (indicated by dotted lines) is more a crescendo of intensity (as mentioned before in the text) than a dynamic one.

Studying this performance in detail (while following the score) will be very rewarding, and playing the recording *many times* will no doubt convince the most skeptical of the value of the arsis-thesis method in acquiring style in playing.

Analysis 5

Emmanuel Chabrier: *Larghetto* for Horn and Orchestra. Mason Jones, *Horn,* and the Philadelphia Orchestra, Eugene Ormandy, *Conductor. First Chair.* Columbia: ML 4629B. This musical excerpt is from the same record quoted above. Jones was a student of Anton Horner (who was also the author's teacher) to whom this book is dedicated.

Jones' meticulous and musical performance over the years has been an inspiration to horn players and musicians everywhere. His musicianship and artistry displayed in this recording shows much evidence of note grouping. The *ad libitum* passage that opens the piece has been chosen as exemplary of the musicality of the entire performance.

EXAMPLE 85

Andante. (A one-movement work.) Measures 6-9.

Even a casual listener can hear the grouping of each two eighth-notes in the first measure. The last two eighths of the first triplet at (3) are beautifully highlighted leading to the gently accented and held **B-flat** at (1). The group at (5) makes the second triplet come alive as the two arses move to the high point in the phrase at (4). A basic rule in musicianship— that one must always hold slightly the first note of every slur —is clearly demonstrated in the playing of the first note at (2), the opening note, **C**, and the **A** in the second measure.

Finally the arsis, **D,** at (6) is played delicately, but it still

has movement into the **C** (the thesis). The fluency and beauty
of motion that Jones exhibits in this performance is remarkable when one remembers that it is basically a slow piece.
Listen also to the *sostenuto* and to the exquisite control that
is evident throughout.

Analysis 6

Johann Nepomuk Hummel: *Concerto for Trumpet in E*
for Trumpet and Chamber Orchestra. Armando Ghitalla,
Trumpet, and the Boston Chamber Ensemble, Pierre
Monteux, *Conductor.* Cambridge: CRS 1918A. This disc is
also difficult to find and is the last recording made by the
great Monteux in this country.

EXAMPLE 86

First movement, *Allegro con spirito.* Measures 66-72.
    The superb musicianship of Armando Ghitalla, principal
trumpet for many years of the Boston Symphony Orchestra,
is the reason for the selection of this example. His note
grouping is outstanding and is easily heard. His complete
command of the trumpet is unequaled and this recording is
one that should be in the library of every serious musician.
He demonstrates in every group and in every measure the importance of note grouping. Listen to this performance many
times and it will thrill you more each time with its life,
musicality and virtuosity.
    Listen, in this short excerpt, to the perfect grouping of
the opening triplet at (5). It is not played 𝅘𝅥𝅯𝅘𝅥𝅯𝅘𝅥𝅯 | 𝅗𝅥 but
𝅘𝅥𝅯𝅘𝅥𝅯𝅘𝅥𝅯 | 𝅗𝅥 ! At (1) the sixteenth is played close to the half-
note. At (2) the two smaller groups are combined in the
larger one (as if in a moderate two beats), yet the smaller
groups are still heard! At (4) listen for the quarter-note

grouping, and at (3) the grouping is perfect, even though the articulations are played exactly as written.

These analyses are only a few examples of note grouping in the playing of acknowledged instrumental masters. They are unusually expressive and have been chosen for their usefulness in helping the uninitiated to grasp quickly the significance of the note-grouping theory. From these excerpts, wherein the performer has gone to great lengths to make the arsis-thesis groups and motives clearly audible, to the type of passage where the artist plays in a strictly rhythmical and metrical manner (without regard for the *expressive* qualities of the music), the gradations are endless.

By much study and listening, however, the reader can soon learn to listen for and identify the expressive quality in music when it occurs by becoming sensitive to the increased or decreased importance of the arsis as the artist plays, and by developing an awareness of the presence of note grouping in the performer's execution.

The author feels that it would be very presumptuous of him to express the thought that these foremost players whose playing has been analyzed above arrived at their interpretive ideas only through the use of the note-grouping method; however the fact remains that their playing *does* reflect the use of a similar treatment of the note groups. One has only to go to concerts or listen to recordings of the great artists to prove this to himself. Whether they are *thinking* along the same lines is an enigma about which one can only speculate. In any case, can one do better than imitate acknowledged masters? Musicianship and style are *learned* attributes. Some may be born with the gift of talent and intelligence and learn very quickly—others more slowly—but *all have to learn*.

In the foreword of *The Grammar of Conducting* by Max Rudolf, George Szell, the late giant of the conducting profession, said of textbooks on conducting:

> . . . It is often assumed that baton technique cannot be taught or learned *systematically*. For this reason textbooks on conducting have been regarded as inadequate means of instruction. Such an attitude is just as fallacious as would be a similar attitude toward textbooks on surgery. Ob-

viously, no one would consider allowing a surgeon to oper-
ate without adequate practical experience. But it is even
less conceivable that a student of surgery could dispense
with a thorough study of textbooks dealing with his special
craft or art.[1]

The purpose of this volume is therefore apparent: to help
the student or professional by *textual means,* in addition to
study with a good teacher and much practical experience, attain the highest degree of artistry that is possible for him.

1. Max Rudolph, *The Grammar of Conducting* (New York:
G. Schirmer, Inc., 1950), p. vii.

8 CONCLUSIONS

Willi Apel, writing on the subject of "Analysis" in the *Harvard Dictionary of Music,* says that "in present day [music] education special emphasis is placed on analysis of harmony and of form; *melodic analysis,* however, perhaps the most important and most informative of all, is usually neglected."[1]

While every educated musician should be well versed in harmonic and formal analysis, these are subjects that primarily concern the composer and the musicologist, and of course the conductor. The performing instrumentalist or singer however is principally occupied with *melody.* Interpreted music without melody is not true music. Nevertheless, strangely enough the average student rarely gets any practical instruction in the analysis of this most critical element of his art, and it is expected that the procedures and ideas set forth in this book will be of aid and assistance in this regard.

Arnold Schönberg has stated that "ideas can only be honored by one who has some of his own; but only he can do

1. Willi Apel, "Analysis," *Harvard Dictionary of Music* (Cambridge: Harvard University Press, 1951), p. 36. (Italics by the author).

honor who deserves honor himself."[2] It is hoped that the reader will have his imagination fired by the concepts expressed in the foregoing pages and will be intrigued enough by their content to continue to develop his own ideas and thoughts concerning them.

In writing of the *Empfindsamkeit* spirit in Germany during the Rococo period of musical history, Lang quotes Carl Philipp Emanuel Bach, Johann Sebastian's famous son, as follows: "Moving performance calls for a good mind capable of subordinating itself to certain common sense rules."[3]

It is realized that in today's world with its many freedoms and in many instances lack of discipline, the above statement sounds rather anachronistic. However to learn to properly execute music, or more specifically melody and rhythm, *with expression and style,* it is felt that both student and professional musician will have to apply the discipline of the "common sense rules" of *melodic movement* to their playing. They will have to follow the example of the master players by analyzing melodies, by listening to performances of the greatest artists, and by practicing *note grouping* until its principles have become a fundamental part of their inner artistic and emotional feelings.

It has been shown that the arsis is the motion-creating, enjoyment-creating factor in music, and that to be expressive, music is dependent upon the arsis being properly played. A method of grouping notes has been presented that demonstrates what might be called a *philosophy of performance* that if understood and *followed,* will help to insure that the importance of the arsis in musical performance will not be ignored. Now, any musician may infuse his performance with a touch of that fleeting and elusive quality called musicianship or style!

If one individual is aided in his efforts to attain this attri-

2. Arnold Schönberg, *Style and Idea* (New York: Philosophical Library, 1950), p. 49.
3. Paul Henry Lang, *Music in Western Civilization* (New York: W. W. Norton and Co., 1941), p. 588.

bute in his playing or singing—one of the most difficult of all the facets of music study to master—the writing of this work has been more than worthwhile. Perhaps it will help performers everywhere to more quickly reach that goal of all art: *THE BEAUTIFUL!*

———————

In a recent TV interview, after he had played a beautiful selection, Isaac Stern, the great violinist, was asked: "When *you* play, the music is so enjoyable and when others play it is so dull! What is it that you do"? Stern replied, "It's what happens *between* the notes!" He then demonstrated, playing first the "dull" way and then the expressive way. The reaction of the audience was spontaneous. This, in essence, is what this book is all about: how to play or sing more expressively, with feeling and emotion, illustrating *"what happens between the notes!"*

BIBLIOGRAPHY

Apel, Willi. *Harvard Dictionary of Music*. Cambridge: Harvard University Press, 1951.

Anciaux, Louis. *Le Rythme, Ses Lois et Leur Application*. Tamines (Belgique): Duculot-Roulin, 1914.

Christiani, Adolph F. *The Principles of Expression in Pianoforte Playing*. New York: Harper and Brothers, 1885.

Dorian, Frederick. *The History of Music in Performance*. New York: W. W. Norton and Co., 1942.

Emmanuel, Maurice. *Histoire de la Langue Musicale*. Vol. II, Paris: Librairie Renouard, 1911.

Ferguson, Donald N. *A History of Musical Thought*. New York: Appleton-Century-Crofts, Inc., 1948.

Finn, William J. *The Conductor Raises His Baton*. New York: Harper and Brothers, 1944.

Gajard, Dom Joseph. *The Rhythm of Plainsong*. Translated by Dom Aldhelm Dean, New York: J. Fischer and Bro., 1945.

Gevaert, Auguste. *Histoire et Théorie de la Musique de l'Antiquité*. Tome II. Gand: Annot-Broeckman, 1881.

Goetschius, Percy. *The Theory and Practice of Tone Relations*. New York: G. Schirmer, Inc., 1892.

Goodchild, Mary Antoine. *Gregorian Chant*. New York: Ginn and Co., 1944.

Grove, George. *Dictionary of Music and Musicians*. Vol. V, Edited by H. C. Colles, 3rd Edition, New York: The Macmillan Co., 1937.

Grove, George. *Dictionary of Music and Musicians.* Vol. III, Edited by H. C. Colles, 4th Edition, Edinburgh: R. and R. Clark, 1940.

Haydon, Glen. *Introduction to Musicology.* New York: Prentice-Hall Inc., 1941.

Idelsohn, A. Z. *Jewish Music in its Historical Development.* New York: Henry Holt and Co., 1929.

Indy, Vincent d'. *Cours de Composition Musicale.* Paris: Durand et Cie, 1912.

Johnstone, J. Alfred. *Touch, Phrasing and Interpretation.* London: William Reeves, 1909.

Lang, Paul Henry. *Music in Western Civilization.* New York: W. W. Norton and Co., 1941.

Leichtentritt, Hugo. *Musical Form.* Cambridge: Harvard University Press, 1951.

Lussy, Mathis. *L'Anacrouse dans la Musique Moderne.* Paris: Librairie Fischbacher, 1903.

Lussy, Mathis. *Musical Expression.* London: Novello and Co., Ltd., 1931.

Matthay, Tobias. *Musical Interpretation.* London: Joseph Williams, 1914.

Mocquereau, Dom André. *Le Nombre Musical Grégorien.* Tome I, Rome, Tournai: Desclée et Cie., 1908.

Mursell, James L. *The Psychology of Music.* New York: W. W. Norton and Co., 1937.

Piston, Walter. *Counterpoint.* New York: W. W. Norton and Co., 1947.

Pratt, Waldo Selden. *The History of Music.* New York: G. Schirmer, Inc., 1927.

Reese, Gustave. *Music in the Middle Ages.* New York: W. W. Norton and Co., 1940.

Riemann, Hugo and Fuchs, Carl. *Practical Guide to the Art of Phrasing.* New York: G. Schirmer, 1890.

Robertson, Alec. *The Interpretation of Plain Chant.* London: Oxford University Press, 1937.

Rudolph, Max. *The Grammar of Conducting.* New York: G. Schirmer, Inc., 1950.

Sachs, Curt. *The Rise of Music in the Ancient World, East and West.* New York: W. W. Norton and Co., 1943.

Saint Saëns, Camille. *On the Execution of Music and Principally of Ancient Music.* San Francisco: Blair-Murdock Co., 1915.

Scherchen, Herman. *Handbook of Conducting.* London: Oxford University Press, 1935.

Schönberg, Arnold. *Style and Idea.* New York: Philosophical Library, 1950.

Stiévenard, Émile. *Essai sur la Prosodie Musicale.* Paris: Menestrel-Heugel, 1924.

Stokowski, Leopold. *Music for All of Us.* New York: Simon and Schuster, 1943.

Ward, Justine. *Gregorian Chant.* Washington: Catholic Education Press, 1923.

Webster's Collegiate Dictionary. 5th Edition, Springfield: G. and C. Merriam Co., 1946.

APPENDIX A
RECOMMENDED
RECORDINGS

It is urged again that the student listen to these and other recordings of foremost virtuosos, *following the score at the same time,* so that he may learn to recognize the use of the arsis-thesis concept. Unless he follows the music as the performer plays, it is more difficult for the novice to hear the grouping of notes.

This list is necessarily short because of lack of space, and because it is intended only as an *introduction* to the *aural* appreciation of the performance of music with the artist playing in *groups* and not in printed patterns. It is only by listening for the note groups, and at the same time analyzing the melody as it unfolds on the printed page, that the student can prove to himself the validity of the ideas and concepts expressed herein.

It should be noted again that some items of this list are not readily available. They can be found in most libraries, however, and are outstanding examples of the note-grouping theory. The recordings are not listed in any particular order, and those analyzed in Chapter 6 are not included although they are highly recommended.

1. Peter Tschaikowsky, *Violin Concerto in D Major,*

Op. 35 (RCA Victor: LSC 2129). Jascha Heifetz, *Violin* and the Chicago Symphony Orchestra, Fritz Reiner, *Conductor*. This or any of the recordings by Heifetz will be valuable listening! Watch and listen for the musicianship! Don't merely "bask" in the sound!

2. *Salon Music.* (Musical Heritage Society, Inc.: MHS 1139). Hans Kann, *Piano.* A collection of favorite piano pieces that exhibit the artist's scintillating and musical use of the anacrusis. The author recommends listening also to many other of the fine artists who perform on the discs of the Society such as Jean-Pierre Rampal, *Flute,* and Maurice André, *Trumpet.*

3. *Sigurd Rascher Plays the Saxophone.* (Award Artist Series: AAS-703). A collection of saxophone solos played by perhaps the most eminent player and teacher of this instrument. In the opinion of the author, the musical expressiveness and beauty of Professor Rascher's playing is due to his delicate and sensitive use of the arsis-thesis approach to melody.

4. *French Horn Masterpieces.* (Boston Records: Chamber Music Series No. L-200). James Stagliano, *Horn,* and Paul Ulanowsky, *Piano.* Listen especially to the *Sonata for Horn and Piano, Op. 17,* by Beethoven.

5. *Cornet Favorites.* (Nonesuch Records: H-71298). Gerard Schwarz, *Cornet,* and William Bolcom, *Piano.* The most *musical* cornet playing the author has heard. A truly great player. Other recordings by Schwarz are available.

6. *60th Anniversary Celebration.* (CBS Masterworks: AE 71226). Isaac Stern, *Violin;* Pinchas Zukerman, *Viola;* Itzhak Perlman, *Violin;* and the New York Philharmonic, Zubin Mehta, *Conductor.* A magnificent performance by three of the most famous string artists of today. Very *musical* playing. *Listen for note grouping while watching the score!*

7. Richard Strauss, *Horn Concerto No. 1 in E-Flat Major, Op. 11.* (Epic: BC 1241). Myron Bloom, *Horn,* and the Cleveland Orchestra, George Szell, *Conductor.* The most

musical rendition of this famous work the author has heard. Strongly recommended for all horn players!

8. Wolfgang Amadeus Mozart, *Piano Concerto No. 12 in A*. K 414. (Phillips: 6599 054). Alfred Brendel, *Piano,* and the Academy of St. Martin-in-the-Fields, Neville Marriner, *Director.* This is undoubtedly the most musical Mozart you will hear. Few pianists have such disciplined control and delicate touch. Of course there is a very obvious adherence to the ideas expressed in the previous chapters. Every group in each passage is like a sparkling gem contributing to the movement of the whole. Listen for the prominence of the arses and the sometimes almost "extinguished" theses! Any of the recordings of Alfred Brendel are exemplary of the ultimate in note-grouping and are highly recommended, especially for pianists!

APPENDIX B
GLOSSARY OF TERMS
Defined as they are used in this book.

Accent. A stress or emphasis upon a certain note to mark its position in the measure, or its relative importance in the musical phrase.

Accidental (Alteration). A sharp, flat, natural, or other alteration (1) placed before a note in the course of a composition, modifying those alterations given in the signature; or (2) placed before a note, the pitch of which may be in doubt.

Anacrusis. The note or *group* of notes which (1) precedes the first beat of a *measure;* or (2) precedes the first note that occurs on a *beat* or unit of a beat. The "pick-up" or "up-beat."

Arsis (Plural, *arses*). A term employed to mean (1) the *second* of two equal notes in duple meter as written or printed, the first of which falls on the first of the measure, beat, or subdivision of a beat in *simple time* (duple meter) ($\frac{2}{4}$, $\frac{2}{2}$); or (2) the *second* and *third* of three equal notes in triple meter, written or printed, the first of which falls on the first of the measure, beat, or subdivision of the beat in *simple* or *compound* time ($\frac{3}{4}$, $\frac{9}{8}$). In a larger sense, *arsis* means the upbeat as opposed to downbeat; or lifting as opposed to dropping the hand when conducting. It can also mean all the notes in a measure *after* the first (See *thesis*).

134

Barline (Bar). A line drawn perpendicularly across the staff to divide it into measures. The term *bar,* as commonly used, is synonymous with measure, but strictly, the bar is the line itself, not the measure it defines; consequently, bar-line, or *barline,* makes it more clear.

Binary (Duple). Meter composed of two basic *beats* or pulses to the measure that are each divisible by two ($\frac{2}{4}$). There can also be *ternary* division of each beat ($\frac{6}{8}$).

Bracket. The symbol ⌐ placed above a note group or pattern to make it immediately apparent to the player or singer.

Cadenza. A cadence; an ornamental passage introduced near the close of a composition or solo, either by the composer or extemporaneously. It is a brilliant technical display, developing themes of the piece, usually appearing before the coda of the first and last movements of the concerto, and after a hold placed over a tonic six-four chord and before the dominant of the final cadence.

Chant. (See *Gregorian Chant*).

Chromaticism (Greek: *chroma,* color). A tone other than those of the diatonic scale of the particular key, i.e., F# in the key of C Major, providing the harmony stays in C. If, however, F# is used to modulate to G major, it is diatonic and *not* a chromaticism.

Concord (Consonance). A harmonious, restful combination of sounds, aesthetically; the opposite of *discord.* Associated with *thesis.*

Counterpoint. The art of adding one or more melodies or parts to a given theme (subject) or melody. Two or more melodies progressing together horizontally.

Discord (Dissonance). A dissonant or inharmonious combination of sounds, aesthetically. In conventional harmony a discord is usually resolved (proceeds to a *concord* in order to satisfy the ear). Associated with *arsis.*

Downbeat. The dropping of the hand or baton of the con-

ductor in beating or marking time; used in the familiar sense
to mean the first beat of the measure.

Execution. Dexterity and skill, either vocal or instrumental;
agility in performance; the act or process of executing or performing a musical composition.

Expression. That aesthetic quality in a composition or performance which appeals to our feelings or emotions; that af-
fective part of music that cannot be written; taste and judge-
ment displayed in performing a work while imparting to it
the sentiment of the composer. That elusive element of music
that creates imagery of movement in the mind of the listener.

Figure. A small group, motive or design of notes, easily
recognized, that forms the building block of a melody or
rhythm. Connotation varies with different authors. (See
motive.)

Gregorian Chant. A type of monophonic, rhythmically free
vocal music or plain-chant sung in unison, and written according to the eight church modes codified by Pope Gregory
I in the sixth century.

Group. Two or more notes grouped together in an *arsis-thesis*
design, bracketed thus: $\ulcorner\text{AT}\urcorner$; and perceived and executed as
a unit in order to achieve a more expressive interpretation of
music.

Harmony. In general, any simultaneous combination of
sounds. The art of combining sounds into chords and
treating those chords according to certain rules. The vertical
treatment of musical sounds as opposed to the horizontal
(melody).

Hymn. A song of praise to God; a short religious lyric poem
set to music and sung principally in church.

Melody. A succession of single tones having the relationship
of a given mode and/or key, and composed of a unified
rhythmical and metrical structure. The principal horizontal
voice in a homophonic composition; an air or song.

Meter. Measure; verse; arrangement of poetic feet, or of

long and short syllables in verse. The basic scheme of note-values and accents in the measure which may remain unaltered throughout a composition or may change periodically, and which serves as a skeleton for the rhythm. Meter has to do with the design of the *measure,* not of the *phrase.*

Method. A course of instruction (instrumental or vocal); a particular system for playing or singing, usually written and endorsed by a master teacher.

Metric Foot. A certain number of syllables constituting a distinct metrical element in a verse. For example an *iambus* is an element (foot) of two syllables—one short, one long (⏑ —).

Monody. A composition for a single voice. The term was originally applied to those solos which were used in the earliest operas and oratorios, *circa* 1600 A.D. Before that time solos did not exist in any large work. *Monody,* in a sense, is related to *homophony* (one voice and accompaniment) as opposed to counterpoint or *polyphony.*

Motion. Motion in music is that quality of performed music which, in the mind of the listener, gives rise to movement imagery or to a feeling of movement. This mental image of movement can be so strong as to cause musculatory contractions, such as tapping of the foot. It cannot be shown on the printed page but exists in the mind of the auditor.

Motive. Two or more notes that together constitute the smallest basic building block of a melody or theme.

Movement. The progression of one note (arsis) to the next note (thesis) in the *note group* or motive, the hearing of which gives rise to movement imagery in the mind; the progression of the entire anacrusis of the phrase to the next thesis as heard by the listener. Also a part or division, complete in itself, of a large musical work, such as a concerto or symphony.

Musicianship. The professional quality in instrumental or vocal performance which shows sound training in musical technique, expression, and interpretation; a combination of talent and knowledge; style in performance.

Notation. The art of expressing music in writing. A procedure for indicating on paper by means of written or printed notes, rests, and symbols the pitch, intensity and duration of musical sounds. Intensity (loudness or dynamics) and mood (tempo) are shown by the use of letters, symbols and words.

Note Grouping. A concept or method of grouping notes in an arsis-thesis group or unit in order to properly emphasize the elemental motives or phrases of a melody with particular respect to the importance of the arsis as a generator of motion and expression. (See *Pattern.*)

Organum. The earliest type of polyphonic music in use from about the ninth to the mid-thirteenth century, usually consisting of two voices, which could be duplicated at the octave, moving in parallel fourths or fifths.

Passage. Any phrase or short section of a melody or composition; a particular component part of a strain or movement.

Pattern. A pattern is understood to mean the metrical arrangement of the smaller notes (note-values) comprising a subdivision of the next larger note as they appear when *written* or *printed* in *beats;* that is, in the succession: *thesis-arsis* (binary division) ($\overline{\text{TA}}$), or *thesis-arsis-arsis* (ternary division) ($\overline{\text{TAA}}$). This arrangement is opposite to that conceived in the note grouping theory which is *arsis-thesis* (binary) ($\overline{\text{AT}}$), or *arsis-arsis-thesis* (ternary) ($\overline{\text{AAT}}$).

Period. A term frequently used to denote a group of measures comprising a natural division of a melody. Usually considered as being composed of two phrases. (See *Phrase.*)

Phrase. A natural division of the melodic line, comparable to a phrase or clause in speech or prose; half of a period. The term is used with so little exactness and uniformity that a more specific description can not be given. It may comprise two, three, four or more measures.

Polyphony. Many-voiced music. Music formed of two or more independent melodies to be played or sung simultaneously; contrapuntal music which originated circa 1200 A.D., and which was developed in the fourteenth, fifteenth, and sixteenth centuries.

Rhythm. The division of musical ideas, motives, phrases or sentences into clearly defined melodic, harmonic or metrical portions; musical accent and cadence as applied to melody. Rhythm represents the regular *pulsations* (not meter) of the music *itself. Rythme* (Fr.) means a half-phrase or part of a phrase. (See *Section.*)

Score. The complete instrumental and vocal parts of a composition, written on separate staves and placed one over the other on the same page to enable one to read each voice of the entire work simultaneously, measure by measure.

Section. Usually applied to one-half of a *phrase.* Used variously by different authors; sometimes composed of two motives or figures. (French: *rythme.*)

Sentence. A complete theme of melody, usually comprising two *periods;* one called *antecedent,* and the other *consequent.*

Sequence. In early liturgical music a sequence denoted the oldest and most important type of literary and musical addition to the *Alleluias.* Usually the addition of text (poetry) to the long vocalizations over the final vowel of the *Alleluia* was provided to facilitate memorization.

Slur. A curved line drawn over or under two or more notes, signifying that they are to be performed *legato* (not separated). Originally it indicated the number of notes to be executed in one stroke of the string player's bow.

Ternary (Triple). Meter composed of three basic beats or pulses to the measure, each divisible by two ($\frac{3}{4}$), or three ($\frac{9}{8}$). Beats and notes themselves also are ternary or binary depending upon whether they are divisible by three or two.

140 *Note Grouping*

Thesis (Plural: *Theses*). The first of two equal notes (binary) or three equal notes (ternary), as *written* or *printed,* that falls on the first of the measure, beat, or subdivision of a beat. In a larger sense, *thesis* means the down beat as opposed to upbeat (arsis); the exhalation of the breath; the fall of the foot in taking a step.

Time. The measure of sounds in regard to their duration; the speed of the notes or rhythm. The rapidity with which the natural accents follow each other (*tempo*). This is the correct meaning of *time;* nevertheless an almost universal custom prevails for using the word *time* to express meter, the division of the measure (*time* signature: $\frac{2}{4}$, $\frac{3}{4}$, etc.); when these are actually *meter* signatures.

Upbeat. The raising of the hand or baton in beating or marking time; used herein to mean the second beat in a $\frac{2}{4}$ measure; the last beat in any measure (before the next downbeat); the anacrusis (arsis).

APPENDIX C
TEXTUAL QUOTES
IN THE ORIGINAL FRENCH[1]

CHAPTER 2

Note 23

. . . au XVIIe siècle la carrure s'installe insolemment: sa vulgarité offre des avantages. Elle jalonne les pas avec une netteté utile aux danseurs. Elle s'accommode à plaisir des percussions initiales—en chaque mesure—dont le danseur est friand.

CHAPTER 3

Note 29

Les *anacrouses* jouent un rôle extraordinaire dans la musique: elles sont l'âme des rythmes et, par conséquent, de l'exécution. Elles ont la faculté de produire *l'accent pathétique,* celle de modifier le mouvement générale, le *dynamisme,* c'est-à-dire la force, les *nuances* d'une phrase musicale et celle de provoquer des *gestes.*

Note 30

Tandis que la théorie moderne ne reconnaît que les mesures *thétiques,* commençant par le frappé et renfermées

1. English translations in the text are by the author.

entre deux barres de mesure, les écrivains antiques admettent aussi des mesures *anacrousiques* commençant par le temps levé. On dirait même que cette dernière combinaison leur ait paru la plus regulière; en effet, ils nomment toujours l'arsis avant la thésis, ce qui, à un certain point de vue, est assez logique, toute percussion étant nécessairement précedée d'un élan.

Note 33
　　Les rythmes commençant sur le temps fort sont relativement rares.

CHAPTER 4

Note 2
　　Dans certains arts, *architecture, sculpture, peinture,* l'ensemble apparaît avant le détail: l'assimilation de l'oeuvre se produit du *général* au *particulier.* Dans les autres, au contraire, littérature, musique, le détail frappe d'abord et conduit à l'appréciation de l'ensemble: l'assimilation se produit de *particulier* au *général.*

Note 5
　　Prendre et rendre, telle est la fonction physiologique de l'homme. La première chose que fait un être in venant au monde, c'est *aspirer,* prendre l'air. La dernière chose qu'il fait c'est *expirer,* rendre la dernier soupir: c'est l'arrêt, le repos suprême!

CHAPTER 6

Note 7
　　Les musiciens modernes reconnaissent que l'utilité de la barre de mesure a été mal comprise depuis deux siècles et que les théoriciens lui ont attribué une fonction qu'elle ne possède pas. La mesure est le moyen mécanique d'exécuter avec précision les durées de notes qui se succèdent.

Note 9
　　En réalité, les mesures n'ont en soi aucune relation avec le sense musical.

APPENDIX D
INDEX OF
MUSICAL EXAMPLES

DATE DUE

Demco, Inc. 38-293

DEMCO